Leading Up
by Joel Mayward

LEADING UP

finding influence in the church
beyond role and experience

joel
mayward

THE YOUTH CARTEL

San Diego, California

Leading Up

Publisher: Mark Oestreicher

Managing Editor: Anne Jackson

Cover Design: Bethany Stolle

Layout: Adam McLane

Creative Director: Napoleon Bonaparte

Scripture quotations marked NLT are taken from the Holy Bible, New Living Translation, Copyright © 1996, 2004, 2007. Used by permission of Tyndale House Publishers, Inc., Carol Stream, Illinois 60188. All rights reserved.

Scripture quotations marked NIV are taken from THE HOLY BIBLE, NEW INTERNATIONAL VERSION®, NIV® Copyright © 1973, 1978, 1984, 2011 by Biblica, Inc.™ Used by permission. All rights reserved worldwide.

ISBN-13: 978-0-9851536-7-0

ISBN-10: 0985153679

The Youth Cartel, LLC

www.theyouthcartel.com

Email: info@theyouthcartel.com

Born in San Diego

Printed in the U.S.A.

Contents

Part 1: The Fable

Leading Up

Introduction

This story is true. That isn't to say the events actually happened or that you could meet up for coffee with any of these characters in real life next week. It's true in the sense that truth is more than facts, and art reflects the truths of reality. On one level, it is a story illustrating principles behind leadership in the church. On another level, it is a glimpse into one young leader's soul as Christ leads him on a journey of trust. May your own soul be encouraged as you learn to listen for the Spirit's voice in these pages.

Chapter One

Failed Ignition

Logan turned the key in the car's ignition, tears forming in the corners of his eyes. The growl of the engine
igniting to life was a stark contrast to his drained spirit.
He felt crushed. The afternoon pastoral staff meeting had
gone from awkward to disaster. He had entered feeling
prepared, even excited. His passion for missions and social justice for Evergreen Community Church came out
in nearly every conversation. His vision for the church
didn't exactly fall in line with the job description of a
junior high pastor, but too many sleepless nights mulling
over the problem meant that he had to take action, if only
to get it out of his system. It was beyond wishful thinking or "what if?" scenarios. He could see that the church
was in desperate need of a change. Maybe he was that
change.

After many hours of prayer and talking over his ideas
with Noah, the high school pastor, Logan felt ready to
communicate his vision. He came into the meeting with
handouts for each pastor and an eager anticipation for
what God was doing at Evergreen. It was a huge moment
as he realized that he could be the head of a revival. It
seemed quite natural that an increased focus on missions
and social justice were exactly where the church needed
to go; Logan was just there to point out the obvious.

"Here's what I've been thinking..." Logan began. That was the beginning of the end.

The lead pastor, Simon, had responded to his suggestions about their church's approach to missions with a quick smile and a "thanks for sharing, Logan" before directing the conversation to something about the need for a better calendaring system for the upcoming summer months. The meeting ended and not another word was said about Logan's ideas. He walked out of the church building alone.

"Calendars! Who cares about the calendars when we're missing a central element to the gospel, when we're ignoring a huge portion of our community for the sake of comfort! For a church with "community" in its name, we seem focused on all the wrong things," Logan thought. During the fifteen-minute drive home, a flood of thoughts and emotions burst out from Logan's heart. A sudden wave of anger swept over him, and he slammed his fist into the dashboard in a fit of rage. Surprised at his bruised hand and dented dashboard, he tried to concentrate on the road in front him. Fuming with a mix of anger and despair, Logan's thoughts drifted to visions of greener pastures, wondering if Evergreen was the right church for him.

The emotions from this botched meeting weren't overdramatic. Logan had tried multiple times before to communicate new ideas to the other pastors over the years—bringing up thoughts at dinners with elder members, sharing new ministry books he was reading with Simon, or offering feedback to Noah about his event calendar. Every conversation seemed to have the same results: a smile, a nod, and "I'll think about it," with little-to-no actual response. He wondered what the other leaders thought of him, speculating that they might all have some sort of negative perception of him. *Why else would they brush me off? What's their problem with me? What did I ever do to them?*

"This is it," he thought as he turned onto the freeway. "I'm hitting my head against a brick wall here. No one is listening -- really listening. Simon's smiles and head nods just don't cut it. That's not action, it's apathy!" He wiped the tears off his cheeks, embarrassed and hoping that other drivers didn't see his pain. The freeway lights washed over the car with a steady rhythm as he raced home.

"And Noah just sat there, quietly watching me go down in flames in front of our entire staff. I thought he was on board with this! I thought he had my back. What happened to 'sounds awesome, Logan, I really think the Lord is moving here, Logan?' If the Lord is moving, then why doesn't anyone else seem to be moving? I love the church, but I just don't know if this church will ever catch the vision. God…what am I supposed to do next?"

Logan sighed as he approached the next exit. The dejection had set in. Normally enthusiastic and passionate, his lonely weeping in the car felt strange, like he suddenly wasn't himself. His once-ignited passion for church ministry was sputtering out.

***

As he pulled into the garage, Logan was surprised to see his wife Ava already home and taking out the garbage. *But where was her car?* No time to think about it. Immediately noticing his reddened eyes and bruised hand as he stepped out of the car, Ava stood quietly and listened while Logan vented his frustrations from the day. It pained her to see her typically optimistic husband spew words of cynicism and defeat. As was a volunteer in his ministry, she had seen the countless hours he had poured into the junior highers and his volunteer team. He had also taken a number of college students under his wing, going beyond his job description out of a desire to see former students remain connected with the body of Christ. Even this morning, Logan had met for coffee with a 21-year-old college student who was eager to begin serving in Evergreen's mid-week gatherings. But for the moment, the gifted leader standing next to her appeared defeated. She led him into the kitchen while he continued to share all the details about the meeting.

"I had a handout prepared for Simon with a proposal about missions, but it never even reached that point in the discussion. I figured my passion and excitement about the idea would have gotten some attention or a semi-interested response, but the longer I spoke, the more Simon seemed to shut down. I kept glancing at Noah, but he was just staring at the table. I couldn't even tell if he was actually listening. I expected…I…I don't know what I expected! But I'm not sure if Simon is even open to the possibility of a new approach with missions. I don't know if he's open to *anything!*"

"Sweetie," Logan continued, "we've been here six years, and I've taken this ministry from literally nothing to a pretty great junior high group. It *kills* me to see these students grow up, move through high school, and end up…nowhere!"

Another deep sigh exited his lungs. *I know, deep down, that any success hasn't been about me.* He was just venting now. Yet he still felt an inner tension. If God had been so active up until now, why had the pastoral meeting and Simon's response been such an enormous letdown? Why hadn't Noah spoken up? How could the leadership remain comfortable with the church's lukewarm level of evangelism and social justice? Ava began to see that Logan's frustration ran deeper than the events of the day. He was beginning to doubt himself as a leader in the church.

They stood in the kitchen, staring into the linoleum floors, looking for any sense of hope. After a few minutes of silence, Ava quietly spoke up.

"I'm so sorry about your day, Logan. I know this means a lot for you. Your sleepless nights have been my sleepless nights too. We've been struggling together, and I'm proud of you for taking a risk. I don't know what else to say. But I'm with you in this, and I'm not convinced that you need to throw in the towel yet."

She paused, wondering if Logan would be able to take her next words of advice as love and encouragement. "But...I wonder if you need some help in this, some more wisdom and clarity from an outside perspective. Maybe you need a new sounding board beyond me, and even Noah - especially if Noah doesn't seem to really have your back. I wonder...if we should have Caleb and Evangeline over for dinner."

Logan glanced up. "You mean...*like tonight?* I just got home, sweetie, this isn't..."

"No, no, no!" Ava interrupted. "Not *tonight*. Tonight, we drown out the day's sorrows in a few big bowls of ice cream," Ava grinned. "But I'll give them a call. We haven't seen them in months."

She saw a relieved smile spread on her husband's face. She knew that Caleb and Evangeline's friendship meant a lot to Logan—it meant tons to her!—and simply having their kind presence might offer some insight into Logan's frustration with the situation at their church.

"Okay. Let's have them over. I think you're right. I need all the help and encouragement I can get right now."

"Great, I'll give them a call tomorrow, see what we can do."

A renewed spirit stemmed in Logan from the mention of ice cream, "Thanks for listening, Ava. Now, how was your day?"

Ava paused, an embarrassed grin now spreading across her face, unsure how to tell her exhausted husband how her car wouldn't start and was stuck in the high school parking lot.

Chapter Two

"So... who wants to change the church?"

"Hello? *Are you with me?*"

Logan blurted the question out abruptly. He still had been thinking about last week's failed staff meeting, particularly Noah's part in it all. Noah had sat there and stared into the conference table while Logan had gone down in flames. Behind closed doors, Noah had sounded supportive of Logan's ideas. At least Logan had assumed all the head nods and "mhmms" were meant as support. Slightly older than Logan, the high school pastor had been a supportive partner in ministry to his energetic junior high pastor compatriot, and was likely to be found quietly reading theology books in his office.

"Excuse me?" The sudden entrance didn't surprise Noah. The question did.

Noah was confused. Logan had burst into his office and plopped down into a chair, clearly bothered and anxious. He sat in silence for a moment, Noah staring at him, perplexed. Then the question came tumbling out.

"Are you with me? Last week at the staff meeting? I shared the ideas we had discussed before, ideas about changing the direction of our church culture. We've agreed that the concept of missions has been just that—a concept, a theory that hasn't been practiced. You knew I would be sharing about this vision with the rest of the team. You know how much this means to me, so why didn't you speak up?" Logan was clearly upset, his voice getting higher with every question.

Calmly, Noah started mentally connecting the pieces—Logan didn't feel supported, and was taking it personally. He nodded slowly in response.

"There's that nodding thing! You've been nodding all along, but you don't say anything. I don't need your nods, I need your voice!" Logan shouted angrily.

"Now, hold up, Logan." Noah was beginning to get agitated. He had not anticipated a confrontation like this, and the sudden accusations raised his guard.

"We've talked about this missions stuff, yes, but you *never* told me you were going to share that vision in the meeting. I didn't know. But clearly you expected me to share something too, something that I didn't know I was supposed to share. So when you come in here accusing me, you've gotta give me a minute to process all this." Their ministry friendship had been fairly solid for the past three years since Noah had taken the position in high school ministry, though the two couldn't have been wired more differently. Where Logan was the first to speak and offer his opinion in a conversation, Noah was often quietly sitting back and nodding, internally processing or daydreaming, depending on the day.

Noah sighed. "I'm with you, Logan. We do ministry together, and I love the friendship we've formed. But you can't come in here accusing me of not doing something I didn't even know I was supposed to do. I'm sorry man, I don't know what to say here."

"Well, if you're 'with me,' it sure doesn't feel like it."

Logan stood and left the room as suddenly as he came, with Noah confused and hurt in his wake.

***

The church office couldn't contain Logan's brooding frustration. He escaped to the local coffee shop a few blocks away. Sitting down at the table, a moment of inspiration entered his mind—*if Simon won't hear my vision for missions at Evergreen, maybe he'll read it.* Taking out his laptop, Logan quickly typed up an email to Simon, attaching his missions proposal and a quick word on the urgency of the situation. He paused and thought for a moment, then added the email addresses of the other pastors and a few of the elders on the board. He quickly pressed the send button before he could change his mind. Maybe if Simon knew all of these people were reading his proposal, something would happen.

Logan's thoughts began to wander. *What if Simon didn't even read the email?* He seemed so adamantly opposed to this kind of change. Logan began to wonder if Simon even had the character qualities to lead this kind of radical vision. He had served under Simon's leadership long enough to see the lead pastor's strengths and weaknesses. Logan appreciated that Simon had taken a risk in hiring such a young pastor to lead the junior high ministry, and he'd been a faithful supporter in the past. *But Simon is getting older. Maybe he's just too tired for this sort of thing. Maybe if he just stepped down and retired, then I could start to bring some healthy changes here.* Logan began to imagine what it would be like to lead the entire church. He'd be one of the youngest lead pastors in their community. But maybe that was the sort of change their church needed. Maybe Logan was the solution to the problem.

"So…who wants to change the church?" he whispered, staring at the computer screen.

"Who're you asking?"

The familiar voice startled Logan out of his daydreaming. Turning, he saw a tall, stocky grey-haired man approaching to sit down in the chair opposite Logan. The man wore a warm grin on his face and had a mischievous look in his grey-blue eyes.

"Caleb! Hey, wow, it's great to see you!"

Caleb shook Logan's hand, forming a firm grip as he set down his coffee on the table. He was a relief for Logan's discouraged heart. Caleb had been Logan's youth pastor and mentor growing up, but the two had lost touch as Logan entered into full-time ministry and Caleb transitioned to an executive role at another church in their city. It had been Caleb's strong recommendation that had sealed the junior high pastor job for Logan at Evergreen. Caleb sometimes felt like a second father, having taken the young leader under his wing years ago and even allowing Logan to live in his home for a year after he had graduated college.

"It's good to see you too, even if you're still drinking that sissy sugar water." Caleb chided. He only drank black espresso—"an Americano, nothing else"—and taunted Logan for his drink of choice—a white mocha with three sugar packets. "That stuff is gonna give you a heart attack one day, son."

"At least mine tastes good! Yours looks like a mud puddle in a cup. Probably tastes worse." Logan dished back. This was a ritual of sorts; the jokes and sarcasm only revealed the deep affection these men had for one another.

"So...who are you asking?" Caleb repeated.

"Asking what?"

"You said, 'who wants to change the church?' just ten seconds ago. And I'm wondering who you're asking. Yourself? That computer? Your coffee?"

"Oh yeah. Well...I guess I'm asking anyone who is willing to change it with me."

Caleb took a long look at Logan. "You've been chewing on something here, huh? You didn't even see me come in; you were so focused on that screen in front of you. What are you working on there?"

Caleb's question opened the floodgates—Logan spent the next thirty minutes pouring out the entire story, from the initial inception of the vision, to the failed staff meeting last week, to his confrontation with Noah that morning, to the email he had just sent to Simon and the other church leaders.

"So I asked that question because I'm wondering, is Simon is even the guy to take our church there? I don't think "change" is part of that guy's vocabulary."

Caleb, who had been patiently listening and nodding, finally interjected with his thoughts. "Yeah, well, that's a pretty harsh judgment to say for the guy who hired the 22-year-old right out of college."

Logan was stunned. He didn't expect that kind of response. Caleb did have a reputation for calling it like he saw it, and it sure didn't take him long in this conversation. Caleb continued:

"Don't get me wrong. I love your vision, and completely agree with the heart behind it. Missions, justice, all that. It's what Evergreen needs. Yet just because the message and vision are God-centered doesn't make your motives and methods God-centered. It sounds to me, Logan, like you're not seeing some of the bridges you've burned."

"…what do you mean?" Logan's defenses were down for the first time that day.

"What I mean is this: you're not leading up. You've made some assumptions about Simon and Noah that might not have any merit whatsoever. Now, I'm not saying they're without fault here, but I do know that you have conceived motives for each of them without really hearing where they're coming from.

"I bet you've been sitting here daydreaming about imaginary conversations that you'd like to have with Noah or Simon. I bet you've conjured up some scenarios where people recognize how incredible you are as a leader at Evergreen, how they're lucky to have you, that Simon and Noah should finally recognize just what you're bringing to the table. While you've been dreaming and pondering about this vision for weeks and months—maybe even years—*they* haven't. They just heard about it, and you're expecting them to instantly catch up with you when you're miles ahead of them in the thought process. And when they don't, you assume that they don't trust or value you. Any of this ringing true?"

Logan was floored. He sat back in his chair and let Caleb's words sink in. A minute of silence passed, though it felt like an eternity. Logan stared into his coffee cup, but Caleb held a firm gaze at Logan's eyes, waiting for his response. Then Logan spoke.

"I think you're right. You usually are with this kind of stuff, and while it sucks to hear it, I think you've got me. Maybe I'm rushing this whole thing. Maybe I'm not even the guy to share this. Maybe I should just scrap the whole idea."

"No, no! That's not what I'm saying. I think your vision is a great one, and even given from God to change your church community. But you've got to learn how to lead up in order for that vision to become a reality."

"You said that phrase earlier—leading up. What'd you mean by that?"

Caleb sat up in his chair. "Tell you what. Ava called Evangeline last week about making dinner plans for Saturday. And while I don't want our time together to be dominated by ministry conversations, leading up isn't something that I can fully explain over a cup of coffee. It's going to take a dinner or two. So let's chat this weekend, and I'll answer any questions you've got. Maybe I can be a sounding board for all your church-changing ideas too."

"That sounds great! Looking forward to it."

Caleb stood up to leave, then turned.

"Oh, and here's one more word of advice: when it comes to sharing a new vision for church transformation, emailing everyone on staff is probably not the best way to share it. That's a great way to get fired, son."

Logan grinned. "Yeah, you're probably right."

"Nah, it's that sugary garbage you're drinking that's making you think like that. If you want to change the church, it's gonna require Jesus, not emails."

***

When he returned to the office to gather some books, Logan made sure to turn by Simon's office and check in after the email. The office was locked and dark. Feeling a strange mixture of anxiety and relief, Logan left for the day, promising to follow up with Simon when the time felt right. At the pastoral staff meeting the following afternoon, Simon never addressed the email.

Chapter Three
Leading Up

"I'm telling you, it was a wolverine."

"Seriously? Do wolverines even live around here?"

"They must, because THAT was a wolverine."

"Honey, I think that was a possum. Wolverines don't typically lay down in front of cars on major roadways."

"It wasn't laying down; it was crouching to pounce! Possums don't have fangs or beady red eyes. You weren't staring it down like I was. I'm telling you. Wolverine."

"Have you been watching too much of the Discovery Channel?"

Logan and Ava were walking to the door of Caleb's home, having a friendly argument over the nature of the animal that had caused Logan to briefly take an off-road course as they came over a hill en route to Caleb's house. The swerve got both of their hearts racing, and the banter was helping calm their nerves before they reached the front porch.

Caleb was already at the door, a big grin on his face.

"Come in, come in! Evangeline is still getting everything prepared, and I've been banished from the kitchen for the moment. Seems I only slow things down in there." Caleb's smile immediately put Logan at ease, and he felt his nerves calm from the near-accident. The dark and winding drive to Caleb and Evangeline's home was a bit of an adventure, as they lived on a large set of acreage on the outskirts of town. The country road was surrounded by a canopy of trees, darkening the path with a green blanket of shade. The longer commute to his church didn't seem to bother Caleb, but Logan always felt like it was a long trip to head out to their home. Yet their home felt just like that: home. It had been a long time since Logan and Ava had been over, and the smell of cooking food, a roaring fireplace, and a tiny hint of vanilla filled the air. Logan and Ava took a seat on the large couch in the living room. The rustic house was cozy, and was always open to anyone who needed it. As empty nesters, the couple had created an atmosphere in their large house that felt full of grace.

"Hello, you two!" Sitting for only a second, Logan and Ava both immediately jumped up as Evangeline came from the kitchen and greeted them each with firm hugs. She was tall and gentle, with sharp blue eyes that revealed a quiet strength behind them. Her warm spirit was a perfect balance to Caleb's quick wit and candid manners.

"It's so good to see you both. It's been too long! Now, who wants to help me in the kitchen to get some of this food ready? Caleb, you're still not allowed; I'm asking them."

Ava and Logan shared a quick glance—they both knew who would be better at serving Evangeline.

"I'll help! What do you need me to do?" Ava again jumped up from the couch. The two women entered the kitchen, and laughter immediately followed.

"I dropped an entire platter of vegetables earlier,"

Caleb admitted when he heard them laugh. "I can handle all the tools in my tool shop without skipping a beat, but hand me some broccoli and I lose all coordination. Really, it's Evangeline's fault; she's the one who asked for help from a klutz like me," Caleb joked.

"Yeah, well. I'm probably no better. Hence my current position in the living room."

"Well, let's at least set the table and make sure the fire stays going. Go grab some of the wood out back and haul it in here. You remember where it's stored."

A short jaunt to the backyard allowed Logan to fill his lungs with the lush air of green trees and bracken ferns. As Logan piled cut logs from the shed into his arms, he flashed back to his conversation with Caleb in the coffee shop. He had been in such a ministry funk, and Caleb seemed to see right through to the heart of the issue. The man had a way with getting right to the point. While some found Caleb's frank demeanor off-putting, Logan found it refreshing—he loved the honesty he found in Caleb, and knew that it stemmed from a love for Christ, not simply an unrefined personality trait.

Upon Logan's return and Caleb's chiding for not carrying more logs, the two couples gathered in the dining room for dinner. An Italian feast was set before them, with a variety of pastas and sauces that could have fed twice as many guests. Caleb poured glasses of red wine while Evangeline directed the younger couple to the various side dishes. Ava and Logan shot a knowing glance at each other in between passing a bowl of salad. *These two definitely knew how to host a dinner.*

"So what's been new in the lives of Ava and Logan?" Evangeline quipped, eager to catch up on their stories after so many months.

The question felt like a pressure valve had been released. The young couple unburdened themselves with all the various troubles they had been experiencing, from the recent car troubles to Ava's busyness with coaching the local high school's volleyball team. Logan began to share about his discontentment with his ministry, and wondered aloud if he and Ava needed to move on to a different church and have a fresh start. Through it all, Caleb and Evangeline listened and asked questions, but this final statement from Logan brought a quick response from Caleb.

"No way you're going to run from this, Logan. You don't walk away, not like this."

"Okay, so what would you have me do, Caleb? I'm not like you. I can't just suck it up and bear through it. I've got plenty of years of ministry ahead of me, and wasting them here seems like…well…a waste!"

Caleb sighed. "No, you're not like me. You're far more naïve." Logan had clearly hit a nerve with his last comment.

Evangeline intervened. "Now, Caleb. Remember for a minute, sweetie. You and I both know what you were like at Logan's age. If you think he's stubborn, just take a look in the mirror." Caleb just grabbed her hand and gave it a squeeze, a smile crossing his lips.

"Yeah, I know. And I want better for him—for you!" He pointed his attention directly at Logan. "You knew that I was a youth pastor at another church before you met me back in high school. That was my first ministry job, right out of seminary. Man, I don't know why they hired a kid like me, but they had to—there wasn't anyone else who was going to take the job. I worked my tail off, trying to prove myself and be the best youth pastor out there. I had books and curriculum and all sorts of new ideas from seminary. I figured I could change the world."

Caleb set down his glass. "I was there for three years before they fired me." Caleb smirked at the memory.

"When they fired me, I was livid. It felt so unexpected, and so unnecessary. To some degree, it was—I wish they had walked alongside me a bit better, guided me through the mistakes I was making. But in hindsight, I think they made the right call. I wasn't only trying to change the world, I was trying to change and influence the church leadership to be more like me. I was convinced that my ideas were the thing God wanted for our church, that if the other pastors and leaders would just hear me out our church would be…I dunno. Something important. And you know, it probably would have. But those weren't my motives. The vision I had wasn't from God; the vision was from me, and I was just asking God to bless it. I would go into the senior pastor's office and just lay out these ideas like I knew what I was talking about. To his credit, he did listen to me those first few times. But after awhile, the only conversations we were having involved me approaching him about how to make our church better. In essence, I was telling him how to do his job. When he called me on it once, I brushed it off as him making a power-play. That was the beginning of the end."

"So after they fired you, what made you stay in ministry?" Logan wondered.

"Because it wasn't about me, Logan. Still isn't. I was a youth pastor, then a discipleship pastor, and now am an executive pastor, and none of those job titles were my own choosing. I didn't set out on a path to become a successful pastor. I just wanted to follow Jesus, and this seems to be where He has led me. The greatest mistake a young leader can make is connecting his identity to his job description, experience, or achievements. Those are all sinking sand; the only foundation worth building an identity upon is Christ alone."

Caleb continued, "When I got fired, I found out who I was, and I didn't like what I saw. There was a guy with a lot of natural strengths and talents and ambition, but my identity's foundation was misplaced. I spent a year in between ministry roles just learning who I was in Christ and centering my entire being on the Gospel. It's the first step in leading up."

"You keep saying 'leading up,'" Logan said. "You said it in the coffeehouse the other day. I still don't quite understand what you mean by it."

Caleb replied, "Leading up is the ability to influence others beyond one's age, experience, or job description. It is leading leaders, even leaders who are also leading you. It's not pushing your agenda on others or trying to manipulate people into doing what you want. It's far deeper than church politics. That's the dysfunctional kind of leadership I used to have, and it's what got me fired. But leading up requires humility, grace, integrity, and a God-given discernment about what He is doing in your church and community. It's not some formula I'm going to give you either. Christ-like leadership can't dwell in the land of formulas. Learning how to truly lead up is going to require some time and patience. It's like the road leading out to our house, you know? It's dark and winding, and requires a bit more awareness to navigate it well. But a firm sense of who you are and where you're heading makes all the difference in the world."

A bell rang from the kitchen.

"Speaking of time and patience, I've been waiting for the blackberry cobbler to be ready," Evangeline interrupted. "Let's clear this stuff from the table, and we'll eat some dessert by the fire. You two can talk ministry and leadership next week over coffee, right?"

"Yeah, sorry Logan. This blackberry cobbler is going to require my undivided attention," Caleb smiled.

The couples cleared the table and ate their cobbler on the couch in front of the fire, talking late into the night about God, family, and the possibility of wolverines living near the area.

Chapter Four

No One Youer than You

"I'm telling you: black coffee. You don't need self-induced diabetes at age 30."

Logan had barely sat down at their table in the coffee shop and Caleb was already poking fun at him.

"Yeah, but my drink *tastes good*. Yours looks like something that comes from the motor of my car."

"Then you need me to take a good look at your car, because something is wrong with it. Motors aren't supposed to drip delicious espresso."

"Seriously, just try adding some sugar to that sludge. It'd be far sweeter."

"I'm sweet enough, aren't I?"

They both smiled at their ritualistic banter. The week since their dinner conversation had been far less tense for Logan. He had taken a step back from promoting his missions ideas to anyone for now, though he was still unsure where he stood with Simon after the email incident. The two hadn't spoken directly to one another, and Logan wondered if it would be awkward to bring up anything now. Focused elsewhere, he had asked Caleb to start meeting on a more consistent basis to glean his wisdom on leading up.

"How has it been going now that you've stopped being so vocal about your missions vision for Evergreen?" Caleb opened with a question. That was one of his greatest strengths—asking questions.

"It's been going better, though it's been rather difficult to hold onto that vision and not let it flounder now that I'm putting it on the backburner."

"Oh, you don't need to put it on the backburner, do you? I'm not asking you to give up your vision, especially if the Lord has placed it there in your heart. That's the key—a vision from the Lord will grow and thrive, while our own self-created visions have rather temporary life spans."

Logan thought for a minute. "Yeah, sure. I'm not trying to leave the vision in the dust, because it's not like it's left my mind or my heart. I'm still convinced that our church needs to live out the mission of the Gospel in our community, and I doubt that conviction is going to disappear. Fade, maybe, while I wait for the right time to bring it up again. But not disappear."

There was a pause in the conversation, Logan was clearly mulling over something in his mind.

"I'm still curious about your story, Caleb," Logan wondered. "What happened? How did you get fired anyway? You hinted at the reason over dinner the other night, but if I'm going to learn anything about leading up, I need to hear from the guy who got fired in the process…before I get myself fired."

Caleb took a long drink from his Americano. "Oh, Logan, it's a long tale. Start drinking your sugar-water before it gets cold. Basically, I didn't know who I was. It was my first full-time role right out of seminary. Evangeline and I had been married for three years, and the prospect of being paid to do youth ministry was a dream

come true. The church had hired me more out of necessity than qualifications—they simply couldn't afford to
pay someone who had more experience. It was an older
leadership team of two other pastors; my presence cut the
median age of the pastors and deacons in half. I didn't
really know what I was doing, but that didn't matter
much—I was a *youth pastor*, and I was going to be the
best youth pastor this church had ever seen.

"I spent the first two years just trying to get my feet
wet, pouring myself into spending time with the teenagers in the church, listening to their stories, building
a ministry that felt like my own. I brought all the new
books and ideas and curriculum I had learned in seminary with me, so it felt like a ministry laboratory where
I could tinker and tweak and refine my youth ministry
skills.

Caleb sipped his coffee. "During all this, I don't think
I cracked open a Bible unless I was prepping or teaching a lesson. Seminary had taught me plenty about the
contents of Scripture; now I wanted to teach others the
information I knew. I think…no, *I know* I was burned out
on reading the Bible. I figured I had spent the last three
years knowing the Bible, so I'd spend the next thirty
teaching teenagers about it. I don't think I had the self-
awareness to really articulate what my thought process
was like back then, but I can see myself clearly enough
now to know what I was doing. No one else really knew
what I was experiencing, though. The other pastors were
the opposite of micro-managers, allowing me tons of
freedom with the youth ministry in the church. If I didn't
push anyone's buttons or burn the building down, they
seemed pretty satisfied."

Logan interrupted. "You said the other day that you had shared some ideas with your senior pastor and that he had called you on your pushy demeanor."

"Yeah, I had spoken up multiple times in staff meetings and in his office behind closed doors, until the day came that he told me I was—and this is a direct quote I will never forget—'lacking in grace and self-awareness.' Man, that ticked me off! I mean, who was this guy, calling me out like that? He didn't even really know me, or at least that's how I felt, because I didn't really know him! I didn't realize that he was only looking out for me and for his church. I didn't know he was showing me he really cared for me in that moment.

"I began talking about his lack of character and leadership behind his back, first to my ministry volunteers and friends, then to students and parents. It was a horrible way to behave, but I didn't know any better—I still didn't know who I was, even though I thought I did. I wasn't praying much, wasn't listening for God's voice through Scripture and wasn't caring about the mission of the church. Eventually, the senior pastor heard the gossip and called me into his office. He rebuked me for my behavior, and I just snapped, chewed him out right there, and stormed out. I won't tell you what I said, but there were some choice four-letter words. The pastors and deacons had a meeting the next day, and I got the boot."

Caleb sighed, leaning back in the chair. Logan could see that he wasn't proud of these moments in his story, but Logan was sure glad to hear them. The Caleb of the past sounded far too similar like the Logan of the present, and Logan was sure that he didn't want his story to take the same route. Caleb sat up and continued.

"So I got fired. And while it was one of the hardest moments of my life, it was also one of the best. The whole experience caused me to rethink who I was, who I am. I began listening for God's voice again in my life—I wasn't busy doing anything else, really. And as I listened, it turned out that God was speaking all along.

"I realized that I had based a significant amount of my identity on who I was not, rather than who I was. I wasn't the senior pastor and didn't have his lack of enthusiasm. I wasn't the deacons and didn't share in their old ways and traditions. I was never wrong. I mean, I was, clearly. But I realized that my identity was built around a false idea that I was somehow the savior of the church, and a savior can't fail, right? Yet when I was fired, the house of cards I called my identity came crashing down around me, and I was left to pick up the pieces."

Caleb suddenly sat up. "You ever read Dr. Seuss?"

"What?" Logan was confused by the shift in conversation.

"Dr. Seuss. You know, the old children's books. He has this quote that has stuck with me over the years. 'Today you are you, that is truer than true. There is no one alive who is youer than you.' Even though it's a bit cheesy, it's right on. There is no one else who has my story, who is created uniquely as me, Caleb. Ephesians puts it this way—you and I are God's workmanship, or masterpiece. The word workmanship means that we are works of art, created by God for His purposes in our lives. And it's all grace—it's all a gift from God.

"Logan, I had to realize through losing my job that my identity could not be found in being a youth pastor. I was not the sum of my job description. Nor was I some sort of self-created masterpiece. Anything I am, anything

I do, anything worthwhile or beautiful or true that comes from me is all a gift from God. But it's a gift of God *through me*, His masterpiece. And that didn't matter if I was an official pastor or not. It's how I could go from being a washed up youth pastor to my second youth ministry job—where I met you—to becoming a discipleship pastor, then an executive pastor, all while holding onto my identity. I didn't somehow sell out when I moved into the executive role; I still have the same passions for the emerging generation and the local church. I just listened for God's voice and tried to discern what He was doing as He continued to shape me."

"Yeah, I wondered how you went from youth ministry to this executive role. It feels like those would be completely different in nature."

"Well, in some ways they are. I play far less dodgeball now." They laughed.

"But, like I said, I am still the same Caleb who is God's workmanship, created in Christ Jesus for good works. Christ defines those good works; I'm just along for the ride. My identity is secure; I'm a child of God, a citizen of the kingdom, a work of art. Getting fired from my ministry job pales in comparison to those truths.

"Once I figured out who I was, I began to understand the kind of influence I could have as a leader. When I had an identity that was solid and grounded, I was defined by who Jesus said I was rather than immediate circumstances. I once read something by a guy named Edwin Friedman who explained it this way: it's the difference between a virus and a healthy cell. A virus has no nucleus, no cell wall. It simply acts on impulse, centering its ability to thrive by attaching itself to whatever

---

* Edwin H. Friedman, *A Failure of Nerve: Leadership in the Age of the Quick Fix* (New York, NY: Seabury Books, 2007)..

is around it. Virus-leadership leads to making decisions from impulse or pleasing everyone around you. It's about self-preservation and fear. On the other hand, a cell has a nucleus and a cell wall. It contains all the information about who it is and its purpose inside of it. It also has the ability to self-differentiate from other cells."

"Wait, self-differentiate? Explain that one."

"Friedman describes self-differentiation as the ability to know where you end and where another begins. It is being able to both know your own unique identity and calling while also being able to engage others within the context of community. So think of any cell - like a heart cell. It knows that it's part of the heart and meant to perform as a heart cell should. It's not a brain cell or a kidney cell; it's a heart cell. Being self-differentiated means that you're not defined by your job description or the unhealthy impulses and influences of others. You maintain presence without capitulating to groupthink or avoiding being in community.

"I had to learn who I was so I could have any sense of presence. The reason I got fired was that I was like a virus, sucking the life out of others because I was pushing my own agenda without regard for another's presence, or even knowing my own. I didn't have a nucleus or a cell wall; Christ had to form those in me.

Caleb drained the last bit of his coffee. He had managed to consume the whole drink throughout the conversation. Logan looked down at his lukewarm mocha, the syrup having separated from the milk looked less-than-appetizing. He grimaced, then glanced up to see a big grin growing on Caleb's face.

"Don't say *anything*," Logan groaned, knowing the jokes about his "sugar water" were filling Caleb's mind.

"What?" Caleb replied sarcastically.

The two got up and walked to their cars. As they walked, Logan was deep in thought about Caleb's story and its significant parallels to his own life. *Where am I missing God's voice?* Did he find his identity and significance in his ministry role, or in his relationship with Christ?

"Thanks for sharing your story," Logan said. "It means a lot, and I appreciate your honesty about the mistakes you've made and what you've learned. I'm just trying not to make the same mistakes!"

"That's why I shared it," Caleb replied. "Hopefully, you won't have to do the same dumb things I did. It all starts with asking, 'who am I, really?' The answer to that question will define everything else."

Caleb turned to put unlock the door to his truck. He had driven this ramshackle truck for as long as Logan had known him. While it looked dilapidated on the outside, the engine simply purred. Caleb had given a lot of work into making the engine of this truck run smoothly. He turned and glanced at Logan.

"Now, you've got youth group with the junior highers tonight, right? Well, I've got the night off. So, I'm coming and crashing your youth group! That comment about dodgeball has me itching for a game. Time to show some of these junior high kids that this old guy still has it in him!"

Caleb struck a pose that was supposed to look athletic and intimidating, but came across looking a bit like he was impersonating a chicken. Logan laughed; the guy couldn't get away from the levity of youth ministry. Maybe it was just part of who he was, and always would be.

Chapter Five

Dual Paradoxes

"I'm sorry."

The scene felt familiar to Noah. Logan walked into the office and plopped down in the chair opposite his. But instead of a brooding posture, Logan was sitting forward with a sheepish smile on his face. He repeated the apology, shaking his head.

"I'm sorry for when I chewed you out a month ago. There's no excuse and it was inappropriate on my part. I judged you wrongly and I'm sorry. Our friendship is worth a lot to me, and I don't want to lose it over my own insecurities."

Noah put down the New Testament commentary he was reading and gave his young friend a long look. He had wondered if Logan had any intention of reconciliation and wrote his actions off as brash and immature. This sudden apology was a breath of fresh air in their relationship. Noah leaned forward.

"I forgive you." Logan smiled at the answer, breathing a sigh of relief. "I really do. And you need to know that I'm with you in this. I've missed our theological conversations about missions and ecclesiology. My office door is open to you any time. Apology accepted."

"Good. I'm glad. Thanks for that." Logan looked relieved.

Noah paused a moment. "Since you're here and we're talking apologies, did you ever talk with Simon about the passive-aggressive email situation?"

Logan sighed. "No, I haven't. I'm not sure I will either. It's been so long, and it's awkward to bring it up now. It's not like we were incredibly close beforehand; he's my boss and I'm his employee, and there's not much else there. We've been cordial since I sent the email, but I'm still keeping my distance from the guy."

Noah's brow furrowed. "Well, just so you know, it's the elephant in the room around here. I think a conversation is coming, and as your friend, I'm praying it goes smoothly."

***

The ten leaders filed into the conference room, picking familiar chairs around the large table in the center. Simon opened the staff meeting in prayer and dove into the meeting's agenda. First, a devotional from Cheryl, the college pastor, who shared about the incarnation of Christ being both fully human and fully God. Logan's mind was wandering as something in Cheryl's remarks caught his attention. She mentioned Jesus' birth in a barn — how He came from such lowly beginnings as a human baby, yet still remaining part of the Triune God.

"How does that work?" Logan blurted out. The rest of the pastors stared at him. Noah stifled a laugh, but Simon looked annoyed. Logan avoided his gaze.

"How does what work?" Cheryl asked, a bit confused by the interruption.

Logan ignored the awkwardness of the moment. "He's both. Jesus, that is. He's God and human, fully sovereign and powerful, yet weak and helpless. He has all the control and none of it at the same time. How does that work?" Logan wasn't really inquiring as much as wondering aloud.

"Well, it's a paradox," Cheryl answered. "It's one of those mysteries about God that we know to be true, yet our minds can't fully wrap around how it's actually possible."

"Yeah, but how does that work *for me*?" Logan wondered.

"I'm not following you. Are you saying you're Jesus?" Cheryl wondered. Everyone laughed at that point, breaking the tension as Logan's internal thoughts found themselves out in the open.

"Sorry. Never mind."

Logan wasn't asking about the incarnation any more; the theological conversation had given language to a question he'd been forming in his mind for weeks. Even as the staff meeting progressed, Logan began scribbling notes into his journal. As soon as the meeting closed, he was swiftly walking to his office, his phone in his hand and Caleb's number on speed-dial.

"Hey, how's life, son? How's your day been going?" Caleb greeted.

"How do you influence leaders without capitulating to either dominance or weakness?"

"Well, hello to you too!"

"Seriously, okay, the idea has been stirring in my mind for awhile now, and I finally figured out the right words to ask the question. Cheryl was talking about the incarnation—you remember Cheryl, she's the college pastor—and I realized that I'm struggling with this tension in leading up between wanting to share my ideas about missions because they're great, but then not wanting to share them out of fear that I'll steamroll others again."

"Yeah, well…it's a paradox, isn't it?"

"I know, but I'm hoping there's a more satisfying answer here than just 'it's a mystery, so accept it.'"

There was a pause on the line. Caleb took a deep breath, gearing up for a long response. Logan's notepad was out, pen in hand.

"When I was in my first youth pastor role, I remember going into the office of my senior pastor, sitting down across from him, and just spewing out idea after idea about how our church needed to get its act together. Really, I was sharing how I thought he needed to get his act together, particularly making sure his leadership was in line with what I was thinking. I thought I was God's gift to his church. But it wasn't anything more than arrogance and pride.

"On the other hand, after I got fired and went to my next church—the one where you and I met—I found myself sitting silently through staff meetings for the first year, not saying a word. My experience from getting fired had instilled a fear inside of me that led to a posture of self-preservation. '*Don't rock the boat and you keep your job.*' I couldn't afford to take another risk like that, either emotionally or financially. So while I still had ideas and input, I kept much of that to myself out of fear that any sign of weakness or dissent would ultimately lead to the loss of my job.

"The thing is, both of those leadership styles are essentially the same. I call it insecure pride. Even though insecurity and pride seem to be opposites, I think they're really two sides of the same coin. The commonality between them is that they're both focused on one's self.

When I'm being prideful and cocky, it's because I'm too focused on my own abilities and how great they are. When I'm anxious and insecure, it's also because I'm too focused on my own abilities, only how incapable they are instead. Pride is a bit more external and boisterous, while insecurity hides in the depths of our hearts and causes leaders to clam up when they should speak up. It took the senior pastor of my second church to ask me to speak up more for me to realize what I was doing. When I was holding on to all these ideas—Spirit-driven ones included—I was actually being disobedient to God's leading in my life, and it was hurting the church.

"Now, the opposite of insecure pride is humble confidence."

"Okay, Caleb, but that sounds pretty much like the same thing to me."

"I know, but it's vastly different. While insecure pride is focused on yourself, having humble confidence comes from focusing *outside* of yourself, finding worth and value entirely in Christ. You know where we get the word 'humble?' It's from the Latin word meaning 'earth' or 'dirt.' Those types of leaders recognized that they're just dirt, that everything they have is attributed to blessing. Yet they are also incredibly driven, not for themselves, but for the mission of the organization. They work incredibly hard, give countless hours, and create thriving organizations.

"Now, think about Jesus. Here is a guy who both washes his disciples' feet and draws crowds of thousands who will hang on His every word. He hangs out with the outcasts and marginalized in society, yet also recognizes that He is a king ushering in a kingdom. His humility stems from His relationship with the Father; He knew who He was and knew what His mission was all about.

Having humble confidence stems from knowing who I am in relation to God. If He has created me and called me to lead, then I need to be faithful to that calling and mission. Yet it's still a calling; it's a *gift*, and it has nothing to do with my own ability."

"My mind just went to where Jesus is described as both the lowliest of servants and the one whom every knee will ultimately bow before as the ultimate king," Logan interjected.

"Exactly. And while no one should be bowing their knee before you, that doesn't mean that God isn't using you as a conduit for His voice and mission, particularly at Evergreen. I can have complete confidence in who I am not because of some self-help book or a pep talk, but because I have confidence in the God who created and called me. And that, paradoxically, leads me to humility. It's the whole message of the gospel, actually— the paradoxical power of the gospel is that it both humbles us and strengthens us, having us realize our brokenness, then acting out of the strength of the Spirit of God inside us."

"Two sides of the same coin. And there are two coins—insecure pride and humble confidence."

"More paradoxes, I know."

"Yeah, but I can wrap my head around these. Thanks, Caleb. I've been scribbling notes this entire time, thanks for your wisdom…and for answering my call!"

Logan closed his phone and thought a moment. He walked out of his office and down the hallway into Simon's office. He stood in the doorway and knocked, bringing Simon to turn around in his chair.

"Sorry about the strange interruptions in staff meeting today," Logan apologized. "I've had a lot going on in the back of my mind, and something Cheryl said triggered a new thought."

"Ah, that's okay. Apology accepted, Logan," said Simon. He smiled and asked Logan what he'd been thinking about.

"Oh, just some ministry ideas, some things I've been pondering for awhile. I'm still working things out in my mind though. I've still got a lot to learn."

"Let me know when you've got some ideas worked out. I'd love to hear them," Simon answered.

For the first time since the fateful staff meeting—maybe the first time ever—Logan truly believed that Simon's words were sincere. "Yeah, okay! I'll keep you posted," he replied, and walked back to his office.

Chapter Six

Winning Friends and Influencing People...Without Being a Jerk

"Honey, where are my keys?" Logan called up the stairs to Ava.

"They're in my purse! I had to move the cars in the garage and I couldn't find my set of keys," Ava called from above. The two of them were still getting used to the busy season of the new school year and the ministry commitments that come with it. The leaves falling in autumn were a welcome respite to the humidity and heat of the summer months, and while the season was busy, it was certainly not as stressful as the previous months. With summer camps and summer volleyball practices over, the new school year welcomed a fresh start.

Logan rummaged through the purse, sifting his way through packs of gum and hair ties until his fingers wrapped around his keychain.

"Okay, honey, I've got to go! I'm meeting up with the new intern, Grace!" Grace was a young woman who attended Trinity, the local Christian college. A number of their undergraduates were volunteers in Logan's junior high ministry, since all of the seniors at the college were required to do an internship. Thus, Logan always had a steady supply of eager young leaders who both wanted to help and needed the internship to graduate.

"Love you! See you for dinner tonight!" Logan grabbed his laptop bag and stepped out into the garage. Turning the key in the ignition, the car roared to life, then died. *Huh. That's not good*, Logan thought, turning the key over again. The car immediately turned over, but as the engine settled, the RPMs were extremely low, leaving the car shuttering uncomfortably. It felt like the car could die again at any moment, but it didn't. Logan drove carefully, a bit anxious at every stoplight while the car idled.

Logan made a quick stop at the bank and the local coffee shop before heading to the office. It was that time of the month right before his check deposited into his checking account, only adding to his anxiety. The lower-than-usual funds in the account led to Logan purchasing an ordinary coffee instead of his typical four-dollar mocha. *This day is starting out just perfect*, Logan thought. *An unreliable car and empty bank account are just what I need.* He shook his head. *Okay, okay, Lord. I know it's all a gift. This stuff doesn't matter. Don't let it affect who you are, Logan.*

He pulled into the church's parking lot and walked into the office. Passing by Simon's open door, he smiled and waved a greeting as Simon glanced up from the email he had been reading, waving briefly in return. Logan stopped at Noah's office to chat about the past Sunday's ministry activities before heading to his own office and setting his bag down.

Logan barely had time to sit down when there was a knock at the open door

"Hello? Are you Logan? Hi, I'm Grace. Remember me?"

Logan stood and shook the hand of the young, enthusiastic woman. He certainly remembered her; they had coffee months ago, right around the same time of the infamous staff meeting. She had impressed him with her eager demeanor, but had waited to finish out the semester at the church she where she had been previously volunteering. Grace wore a big smile on her face as she sat on Logan's couch, tossing her purse to the side and drawing up her feet to sit cross-legged. She brushed her long brown hair out of her face and took a sip of the coffee she had brought along. Logan leaned back in his office chair.

"So, how is life at Trinity? How long have you been there now?"

"It's great! Even though I'm a senior, this is only my third semester here. I finished up my Associate's in a community college, and then knew that I wanted to finish up my Bachelor's at a Christian college. This was the closest one to where I'm from—Ashland, it's a small town a few hours from here—so I registered, packed up, and moved out here! That's it in a nutshell, I guess."

Grace talked quickly, but Logan could tell that she was thoughtful. She came off as certain in her words without being arrogant or flippant. *Humble confidence*, Logan thought.

"Awesome. Tell me about your experience with youth ministry, and what you're hoping this internship will look like."

"Well, I grew up going to church, and was very plugged into my youth group. I've always loved music, and picked up the guitar early on. My dad has a background in jazz, so he taught me everything I know. When I was a freshman in high school, I asked our youth pastor if I could help lead worship, and he let me take over the youth worship band, which was a pretty intimidating thing for a freshman. Anyway, I fell in love with it. Not just music, but ministry. I loved leading my friends in worship and loved connecting with the younger girls in our group. When I graduated from high school, I just stayed around and finished up community college while leading worship for the youth ministry. And now that I've been here for a year, I'm dying to really get plugged in somewhere and keep growing."

"Haven't you been volunteering in another church for awhile now?"

"I did, for the past year. I went to my roommate's church, but it just wasn't quite for me. I grew up in a smaller church, and her church has a few thousand people in it. I felt lost, and I didn't ever get to know the youth pastor. I'm not sure he even could remember my name at times, there were so many people he was trying to lead. I wasn't fully using my gifts or passions, and the whole thing felt...stale, I guess. Plus, there were so many other Trinity students that an internship at that church was unlikely. I prayed about it for a few weeks, talked with a few other friends and my dad, and applied here!"

"You and your dad seem to have a pretty great relationship, huh."

Grace sat back for a moment, clearly thinking about the statement.

"Yeah, well. My mom passed away suddenly when I was three years old, and my dad found himself as a single guy with a daughter. We had to figure out life together, and I guess that is one of those make-or-break moments in life."

Grace paused again, tears forming in the corners of her eyes.

"I hardly remember my mom, but my dad tells me that my laugh sounds just like hers." She sniffed. "I'm sorry, that's a lot to throw at you at once. Didn't mean to share too much. I hope that's okay."

"No, no! I asked, and I'm glad you were sincere. Thanks for sharing that part of your story, I appreciate your authenticity."

Logan glanced at Grace's application on his desk. She was confident and mature for her age, and still had a youthful eagerness that seemed balanced with a wisdom learned through hardship. Growing up without a mom required her to grow up quickly. The two talked details about the application for a few more minutes, but Logan had already made his decision.

"Well, Grace, I'm liking what I see here, and we really do need to create a better environment for worship in our junior high ministry. If you're up for it, I'd love you to be our junior high intern! Can you start tomorrow?"

A huge smile filled Grace's face, and she bounced up and down a little on the couch in excitement.

"Yes, yes! Thank you, thanks so much! I'm so ready to get back into ministry, and I can't wait to see what God's going to do here!"

Me too, thought Logan. *What are you up to, Lord?*

***

The car pulled into the long driveway, still experiencing the low idle from earlier in the week. Logan and

Ava got out, grabbing the bottle of wine and a bouquet of flowers from the back seat. Caleb and Evangeline had invited them over for dinner again, and this was an encouraging end to a wonderful week of ministry. Grace's first junior high worship experience showed enormous potential. She had clearly taken time to prepare, and the students responded to her energy in leading and singing. It takes a special leader to get junior highers focused on anything, and Grace seemed to have the gift. Plus, Grace and Ava had hit it off, talking for an hour after youth group had ended and setting up a coffee date that Ava had come from directly before meeting up with Logan for the long drive through the woods.

"Welcome! Let me grab all that from you!" Caleb took the bouquet and wine and headed back towards the kitchen. Logan and Ava followed, moving through the kitchen and ending up on the back patio, where Evangeline and Caleb had set up an incredible spread next to their fire pit. The night was cool but not cold, and the conversation and atmosphere were refreshing for the two couples. Ava shared about the details of her volleyball team's current status as they competed in the regional championships, as well as the potential mentorship she had found in Grace.

"She's got such an energy and excitement for ministry, and our coffee date yesterday went really great," Ava said. "I mean, we've had a few interns come and go through the ministry, but there's some sort of connection or chemistry here, like I know I'm supposed to come alongside her."

"And it's great to have that personal connection with Ava for my relationship with the interns," Logan added. "She brings a lot to the table, especially when it comes to mentoring young women. I don't exactly have a lot of experience knowing what it's like to be a woman." They all laughed. "But Grace adds a freshness to the ministry, and it's been really fun, considering my other relationships with the pastoral team."

"How are those going?" Caleb asked. "What have the past few weeks been like for you?"

"It's been better, both as in 'the past was better' and 'it's getting better.'" Logan paused at what he had just said. "I have no idea if that makes sense, but…it's better."

"How can you tell if things are really getting better with those relationships, particularly with Simon? What's your standard for better?"

Logan paused, processing the question. What *did* it mean to have a better relationship with the team? What had really changed? And if there was change, was it actually better?

"Well, I suppose it has to do with how we've been interacting with each other. There hasn't been any conflict lately, especially around sharing the mission and justice ideas. So that feels better."

"Yeah, it could. But the absence of conflict doesn't necessarily mean that your relationship is deeper or healthier. In fact, conflict is a necessity to relational trust. To overcome conflict together in healthy and beneficial ways is a sign of a good relationship."

Ava jumped in, "Well, Logan has been coming home looking far less defeated. He hasn't slammed his hand into any dashboards lately. That seems like it's better, too." Logan smiled at his wife.

"Okay, so you're feeling fine when you're done with your day," Caleb said. "But is that because relationships are truly better, or because you've just avoided any relationships that could be potentially frustrating? If you keep Simon at a safe distance, you'll probably feel fine for a while. But avoiding conflict might catch up to you."

Caleb paused to think, and then calmly directed a statement towards Logan. "In fact, the way it sounds to me, you're just being a jerk."

Logan nearly spit out his drink. Evangeline playfully punched Caleb's arm, who was clearly unapologetic for his remark. There wasn't a hint of sarcasm or humor behind the statement; Caleb meant it.

"What? It's true," Caleb defended. "If you're just avoiding others and disengaging relationally from people who are part of your team—and part of fostering the changes in the church God wants to happen—then you look nice on the outside, but really, you're kind of being a jerk.

Caleb leaned forward. He was just getting started. "If you're just trying to be nice, stop it. God never calls leaders to be nice. In fact, you won't even find that word in the Bible. 'Love' and 'kindness' and "grace,' but never 'nice.' Being nice has more to do with trying to avoid awkwardness and fostering a good reputation with others. The motivations behind being nice are quite selfish, actually. If you still want to lead up, you've got to learn how to make friends and influence people…without being a jerk."

"Alright, Caleb, thanks for the 'encouragement.' Glad to see you're taking your own advice on this one by creating some conflict." Logan muttered.

"I'm sorry, I'm sorry, this probably isn't the time to bring this stuff up, but hear me out—I'm not saying this because I think of you less, but because I see more in you." The older man raised his hands in a posture of embrace and surrender. "I love you, Logan, and I see the potential you have in the Lord. You've asked me to speak into your life, and we've built a solid friendship. So when I'm telling you this hard truth, know that it's motivated by love and a desire to see you grow. I'm just making a withdrawal on the relational equity I've built with you over the past season."

"What do you mean, a withdrawal?"

Caleb took a breath, a twinkle in his eye now. "Imagine that every one of your relationships in life is like a bank account. You fill up that bank account through the quality time and energy you've spent in that relationship. Everything you do will either increase or decrease your account, depending on your actions, tone, and motives. Just like a bank, when you invest into a relationship, equity builds over time, and with interest. You spend lots of time partnering with someone on a project, make it a point to meet with them on a weekly basis, or use your words to sincerely praise them to others—you're building that equity. A person has far more equity with friends, co-workers, and family than they would with a perfect stranger.

"You can also lose your equity rather quickly by breaking relational trust with a person. It's like having a relational stock market crash. Show up late to every meeting you have with them, share a secret that they've told you, gossip about them, or deliberately sin against them, and you'll find yourself relationally broke.

"Every so often, you'll need to make a withdrawal from your relational bank account. You're going to have to say something difficult or make a hard choice in order to see a vision furthered or a relationship mature. For instance, you might have to call someone a jerk right in front of their spouse in order to see them become a better leader." Everyone laughed, including Logan.

Caleb continued, "See, I can say stuff like that with you and know that our friendship will survive because we've built equity with each other over a long period of time. If you haven't built much equity over time, then the amount of the withdrawal will have less of an impact on your vision and a far more negative impact on the relationship. And there isn't a very good way to fast-track building equity; it just takes time and patience and intentionality and wisdom. It also takes wisdom to know when you can make a withdrawal and not have it bankrupt the relationship. I know I can say hard things to you and even hurt you in the process without destroying our friendship. I made a withdrawal, which was a risk, but it was done out of love, and I hope you can forgive me for any way I've hurt you."

"No, you're right. And to be honest, I wouldn't have it any other way. I love our friendship and the wisdom you're willing to share with me. Even the hard stuff." Logan smiled. "So I forgive you, even though there's really nothing to forgive."

Caleb grinned in return. "Now, to come back to my original question—how are your relationships going with the pastoral team?"

Logan took a moment to think before answering, "They're better. But truly *better*. I've apologized to both Noah for my angry outbursts, and have been making a point to check in with him a few times each week, with no other agenda besides rebuilding that relational connection…or *equity*, now that I think about it." He didn't mention anything about Simon.

Caleb sat up in his seat and leaned in. "That's really important, isn't it? Having an agenda for building the relationship is like that movie, *Inception*. Did you ever see that? There are these thieves who enter into people's minds through their dreams, setting up elaborate worlds and schemes in order to infiltrate the victim's darkest secrets and steal them for themselves. A new client offers a proposal to these thieves—inception, or planting of an idea in someone's mind in order to get them to do what the client wants. Building relational equity cannot be like inception. It can't be about trying to build a personal platform in order to plant your ideas in others' minds. The motivation must be love and mutual encouragement, not to push your own agenda."

Logan began to respond with another question but Evangeline interrupted. "Okay, that's enough talk about inceptions and equity and why Logan is a jerk, so let me make a deposit in each of your relational bank accounts in the form of dessert. I've got another cobbler warming in the oven and it's not going to eat itself."

***

"Well, that got pretty intense," Ava said as she closed the car door while Logan turned the key. The engine repeated its false start from earlier that day, dying only seconds after the key turned.

In a flash, Logan slammed his hand into the dashboard again, cracking some of the plastic. Ava flinched and cried out, startled at her husband's outburst. Logan pulled back his hand, rubbing the outside and looking a bit stunned. They sat silently for a minute.

"Honey…" Ava interjected. "Talk with me."

"I…I'm sorry," Logan replied. "I just…I'm just tired of things going wrong. This car. Simon. The missions stuff. None of it seems to work, and I'm wondering if it ever will. I haven't talked with Simon, and I know I should, but shouldn't he want to talk with me? He's the head guy, the boss, right? I'm just so fed up, I guess, and

Caleb's "teachable moments" sometimes get old. Like, I respect the guy a ton, and I love that he speaks into my life, but I feel like there are so many lessons I have to learn. And this car…this car."

Logan sighed. "I'm so sorry, I didn't realize that I had this bottled up. I didn't expect any of this."

Ava listened quietly. Then she reached over and turned the key in the ignition. The engine sputtered to life.

"It's okay," she whispered. "Let's go home."

Chapter Seven

Cow Tipping

The fall season had given way to the grey skies and chilly mornings of winter. The weeks leading to Christmas were always enjoyable ones, and Logan and Ava were able to spend a great deal of time with their extended family over the Thanksgiving weekend. While the heating system had gone out in one of their cars, Logan was surprisingly unfazed. Ava had a noticed a slow change in her husband since his outburst in the car. It wasn't that he had changed dramatically or become a new person; he was still Logan, but he was a better Logan, with a deeper sense of joy and confidence than she had seen in the past.

His vision for missions and social justice was still in the forefront of his mind, but it had taken a new shape. Instead of a naively youthful passion, Logan now seemed to have a resolve about the vision that was being connected to his actions. During the semester, he had spent far more time out of the office and in the community than ever before, choosing to volunteer as a tutor at a local junior high and turning the local coffee shop into his regular workspace. He was still regularly meeting with Caleb, who still chided him for his coffee preferences. Logan felt like he was becoming a better pastor and leader, that he was on the cusp of a tipping point in his leadership capacity.

Logan had been pondering the implications of the Christmas season. After all, it was a season of joy and giving, and a time of year when many in their community needed significant help. Their church had always given away presents to families in need within their own church, but Logan wondered about expanding that idea to the surrounding neighborhood. Now sitting in Simon's office, Logan stared out the window at the falling rain as he awaited Simon to finish up a phone call. Logan had prayerfully discerned that this Christmas season was a time to share a bit more about his vision for loving their neighbors as a church.

"Okay, sorry about that, just another issue with the heating in children's classrooms that needs to be fixed by Sunday." Simon sighed. The Christmas season was a mixed bag for him, filled with both joy and stress as the expectations and responsibilities seemed to dramatically increase for his role in the church.

"You wanted to talk about Christmas and the gift drive we're doing."

Logan leaned forward, keeping a steady and gracious tone in his proposal. "Yeah, I've been thinking and praying a lot about the gift drive and what it could look like this year. We've been doing it every year since I've been here, and we've always focused on the needs of the families in our church body. I love that, and love that it emphasizes giving in a season where consumerism can quickly overtake the message of Christ's love and sacrifice for us."

Logan took a breath. "But, I also wonder if we could try something new, if we could experiment with giving *more*. The more I've spent time at the junior high school and had conversations with parents and families in our neighborhoods, the more I've seen how many families are really financially struggling this year. What do you think it would look like to expand our gift drive to families in the community who are in need? Instead of a few families, what if we did a gift drive for a few hundred families? Think of the impact that could have in our neighborhoods for the kingdom of God."

Simon thought a moment, and gave his response. "I hear you, and I'm all for giving to people in need, yet I'm not sure if that's the best idea for this year, Logan. The gift drive requires a big sacrifice from our people every year, and like you said, a lot of families are already financially struggling. To ask them to give more... it could actually hurt our families who feel obligated to give, or look pretty awful if we promised a neighborhood family some gifts and didn't come through. I'm sorry, Logan. I love the idea, I really do, but I'm not sure this is the year for it. We've just always done it this way."

Logan sat back, stunned. It had happened again; he had shared a vision, and the idea was over before it started. The two talked a bit more about the Christmas season's schedule and Logan's vacation plans, but Logan's heart was elsewhere.

Ten minutes later, he was on the phone with Caleb, pouring out his frustration.

"I can't believe this, Caleb. The gift drive is such a significant opportunity for our church to really meet a tangible need in the community, but we're just going to play it safe this year! The gift drive has been *exactly* the same every year, and any notion of change just gets shut down. I just can't wrap my mind around it. It was like Simon had already heard the idea before and knew exactly what he was going to say," Logan fumed.

"Have you considered that he *has* heard this idea before?" Caleb asked.

"What do you mean?"

"Maybe he knew what his response would be because he has seen this before. You're dealing with sacred cows here, Logan. Those are always the most difficult cows to tip over."

"Sacred cows?"

"Yeah, sacred cows. These are the ideas, programs, and values that are somehow considered immune from questioning, criticism, or change. Sacred cows are those things that, when questioned, bring up the response of 'we've always done it this way!' They are often unspoken and almost overlooked until someone points them out or questions them. You may have bumped up against one in the gift drive."

"Hmmm…you might be right. But the gift drive isn't bad, per se."

"Oh, I'm not saying that sacred cows are inherently wrong or sinful. They often began as a really good idea or program that slowly turned into something with a life of its own. The gift drive isn't the problem; the underlying belief that it cannot be changed or questioned is where things get unhealthy."

"Okay, so how do I kill a sacred cow?"

"Well, we're not trying to kill it; we're just trying to point out that it isn't quite as sacred as it may seem. If you try to kill a sacred cow, you're going to have a mob of angry cow worshippers asking for your head on a silver platter. That's a great way to lose your job unnecessarily. Sure, sometimes that's exactly what needs to happen; sometimes the status quo needs a prophetic voice to question it, regardless of the personal sacrifice that comes from questioning the norms and values of a culture or organization. Think of the prophets in the Old Testament, or John the Baptist, or Jesus. These guys weren't afraid of scared cows.

"But there is an alternative to killing a sacred cow, especially a beneficial cow that might not need killing. You simply tip it over, revealing that it wasn't quite as sacred as people thought. You both recognize the sacredness that this cow has had in the past, and offer an alternative—and better—future. There will still be naysayers, but it's hard to worship a cow that is lying on its side. Jesus did this too. The entire Sermon on the Mount is an alternative future for the kingdom of God, one that tipped over common religious thought and offered a new way of life."

"Alright, so what would 'sacred cow tipping' look like in my circumstances? I've already spoken with Simon, already proposed an alternative future. That didn't seem to work. And I can't just preach the Sermon on the Mount here."

"Like I said, I wonder if Simon has heard this alternative future before. Or perhaps even experienced it, and it didn't work. Behind every sacred cow, there is a long history. Learn that history, know what alternative futures have been met with resistance, and show why your vision truly is different and new."

Logan heard what sounded like chewing on the other side of the phone.

"Are you...eating?" he wondered.

"Yeah, a homemade double bacon cheeseburger with Swiss. It's delicious. You go tip your cows while I eat this cow for lunch."

***

The same afternoon, Logan was back in Simon's office.

"I heard and respect your decision this morning about the gift drive, but I need your help in understanding how that decision was made. I don't want to step on your toes, and this isn't a question of your leadership more than it is a question about the gift drive. I get the sense that you may have heard this idea before, or that there is something deeper behind why you believe we can't expand the program to our neighborhoods."

Simon leaned back in his chair, staring at the ceiling, clearly deep in thought. He looked like he was debating how to respond to Logan's inquiry. There was a minute of silence before Simon leaned forward and spoke.

"I think there's more to the gift drive that you'd need to hear from me to know why I responded the way I did. Now, I don't feel questioned, at least not in a negative way. This is good, because it's forcing me to process the history behind this thing, and why the thought of changing it brings up sour memories for me.

"The gift drive has been going on for about twelve years now, and it was started by an idea from an associate pastor who helped me plant Evergreen. His name was Tom, and he was a dear partner in ministry. We had this idea for the gift drive to help our people and really exhibit an Acts 2 kind of mentality. We wanted to show that all we had was a gift from God that it was supposed to be used to bless others. So that was the vision behind it for the first three years. But something happened in the third year. Tom and I had been having some disagreements about a few things—the nature of small groups in our church and the way we did outreach. Some of those conversations got pretty heated, but I loved Tom and I thought he loved me, so I assumed we would come out of it just fine.

"One day, right around Christmas and the beginning of the gift drive, Tom comes to me and tells me that he's been talking with a group of our congregants who don't like the direction I've been taking the church. He says that I've been thinking too small, that we need to expand and grow, and this involves a new worship center and a big marketing push in our community. He also says that these people all agree I'm not the guy to lead them into this new season, and that it'd be better for the entire kingdom if I would take a step back and let him lead. One of the changes he mentioned involved turning the gift drive into the kickoff for a building campaign."

There were tears forming in the corner of Simon's eyes as he continued. "I was completely blindsided. Tom was one of my closest ministry friends, and he suddenly made a power play and tried to give me the axe. Man, he was ambitious, had the whole thing figured out and the right people to back him up. The next few weeks were a living hell for me, with phone calls and late night meetings and trying to come to an understanding of the truth, trying to prevent a church split. Eventually, Tom left the church, along with a few of his followers. I don't hear from him much any more, though our kids are still friends."

Simon sighed. "The gift drive the next year was one of the largest we'd ever had, and the impact dramatically changed the life of the church. People's generosity expanded from giving gifts to giving their lives to one another, and we really had an Acts 2 environment for the first time. If we had stopped the drive and done a building campaign, I can only imagine what would have happened.

"I'll be honest, Logan—I fear changing the gift drive because I don't want you to be another Tom. I don't want to lose one of the best programs our church does every year, and I don't want to lose you as a pastor. The email you sent a few months ago—I haven't forgotten about it. I should have addressed it with you then, but I could only think of the awful conversations with Tom, and couldn't go through with it. So I didn't. I'm sorry. I really don't want to lose you. I care about our church—and about our relationship—too much. So, I suppose I'm afraid of what could happen, because I've seen what this sort of proposed change has done before. I can't go through that again. And when I think about the gift drive…I both think about the loss of that relationship, and when times were better with Tom."

Logan was silent. The weightiness of the moment was palpable; this was a holy conversation for the two of them. The history behind the gift drive was far more than presents at Christmas. The program represented the ongoing life of the church through Simon's leadership, the fruit that resulted from a harsh season of betrayal and division. For the first time since coming to the church, Logan felt like he could follow Simon anywhere. Here was a leader who was willing to admit his own fears and brokenness, yet continue to shepherd his church out of a deep trust that God knew what He was doing.

Logan spoke.

"I didn't know, Simon. You need to hear this from me: I have no plans of stabbing you in the back or trying to take over the church. Maybe a year ago the old Logan—the Logan that sent that passive-aggressive email--would have been more inclined to quit or make a power play. But I'm realizing that I don't want to be that Logan, and that God seems to be breaking away those parts of my identity that find value in getting my own agenda across. My heart behind changing the gift drive has nothing to do with a hidden agenda or me. I felt compelled to share it with you because I see what God is doing in our neighborhoods, and I want us—*all of us*—to be on board with His mission. So you need to know that I'm with you, that I'm sorry I haven't spoken with you sooner, and that I'm sorry you went through that with Tom."

"I appreciate that, Logan, I really do." Simon's eyes were still wet with emotion. "I'll be honest too; it's just a bit too late in the season to make that sort of a significant shift in our gift drive now. But I'm serious when I say that we should consider it for next Christmas. I don't want this gift drive to become a sacred cow at our church."

Logan smiled at the acknowledgement of the sacred cow, knowing that the tipping of a sacred cow had turned into a sacred conversation between two pastors and friends.

Chapter Eight
Poking Wholes

"Thanks for coming and serving! So glad you were here!" Logan called.

The last junior high student piled into the minivan and drove away from the food bank. The Saturday morning had flown by for the group as they sorted through boxes of donated food and packed bag lunches for the homeless community. Logan had experimented combining his passion for young people and local missions into this monthly Saturday gathering. The first outing had been a handful of students and their parents, but had turned into a group so large that the food bank was rushed to find jobs for all those eager to serve.

These mornings were both exhausting and satisfying for Logan. It had been a whole year since he had pounded his fist into the dashboard of his car after the failed pastoral meeting. On the outside, not much had changed in their church programs or practices. But internally, Logan felt like a new man. Practicing a posture of humble confidence had led to this initiative with the food bank. He hadn't set out to create a new program in his ministry, but this food bank thing was turning into something bigger than he had ever expected. People surprisingly were eager to serve their community. *What are you up to, Lord?* Logan wondered, a spontaneous smile on his face. He jumped into his car, turned the ignition, called Ava to let her know that the morning had gone well, and headed out to meet Caleb for lunch.

The Mexican restaurant where they were meeting was near the food bank, so Logan didn't have to drive far. Logan arrived and saw that Caleb's truck was already parked out front. The place was a hole in the wall; you could completely miss it if you weren't looking for it. Logan walked through the grungy front door and scanned the place, spotting Caleb in booth near the back. Caleb waved him over and Logan slid into the brown vinyl seat.

"Where did you find this place?" Logan asked. "I hope the food tastes better than this place looks."

"Trust me. It's hit and miss, but when it's good, it's *really* good."

"And when it's a 'miss' instead of a 'hit?'"

"You get food poisoning," Caleb smirked. "But that's only happened to me once. Try the carne asada tacos. They're delicious."

Logan could only laugh. The two men ordered, and sat back to catch up while they waited for their tacos to arrive.

"How was the food bank this morning?" Caleb asked.

"It was good. One of the new seventh graders showed up with one of her friends from school, which was an unexpected blessing. Ryan, the drummer for the worship band, managed to drop an entire box of mustard down a set of stairs, so he and a few others spent most of the morning scrubbing yellow off the walls. Grace was amazing, going around to talk with students and making sure they stayed on task. She does that sort of thing so naturally, balancing the relational side of ministry with the discipline of making sure things get done. She continues to impress me."

"How has Ava been doing connecting with Grace?"

"That's been such a natural thing, too. They're regularly meeting for coffee during the week, and Grace has been showing up to Ava's volleyball practices to help in any way she can. It's like Grace is the little sister Ava never had. It feels like a great relationship."

"I think having Ava be a part of Grace's life allows them both to grow more together than apart. No offense, but I'm sure Grace is getting far more out of her internship by spending time with Ava than with you."

Logan smiled at the light jab. "Yeah, you're probably right."

The food arrived. The conversation paused while the two men consumed copious amounts of salsa and carne asada. As he chewed his tacos, Logan kept thinking about how great the morning was. *Why couldn't this be part of the missions vision I've been wanting to tell Simon? What if our whole church began serving at the food bank?* His thoughts began to race with all sorts of new local missions initiatives.

"You're thinking about something." Caleb interrupted Logan's thoughts. "I can tell, you've got that look on your face, and I don't think it's the tacos."

"Yeah, I'm just thinking about this morning at the food bank and about how great that's going. I'm wondering if it could be more of a whole-church movement. Like, what if we canceled church services for one Sunday? What if 'church service' meant exactly that for one weekend: a church that engages in service? Children, students, whole families could serve alongside each other. I dunno…what do you think of that idea? What if we did that next month?"

Caleb thought a moment, silently chewing his last taco.

"I think your idea is fantastic. Seriously, I love it. I also think that if you did it next month, it would fail."

"Okay, so what am I missing here?" Logan asked. "If it's such a good idea and makes sense, why not just go for it?"

Caleb swallowed and shared a story. "Years ago, I remember talking with one of my friends who had just graduated from seminary. He jumped into a new role as a senior pastor at a smaller rural church, mostly with elderly people. It was his first role, and he was so excited to implement all of the ideas he had learned at seminary in this church. He shows up the first week and looks around the sanctuary, and the first thing he notices is the stained glass Jesus on the stage. Seriously, almost the entire back wall of the sanctuary was a glass mosaic of Jesus, with the sun gleaning through and casting a rainbow of colors over the front half of the room. My friend takes one look at this thing and thinks, 'Wow. That's ugly and distracting.' He asks the janitor at the church if they had a curtain, and the two of them manage to string up a large black curtain left over from a production years earlier. Stained glass Jesus now has a blanket.

"The first Sunday, the congregants come into the room, and there are audible gasps in the room. The worship felt stilted and awkward, and my friend noticed that a large number of folks were actually glaring at him while he preached his first sermon. When the service closed, he found one of the elders at the church and asked him why the service felt so terrible. The man proceeded to tell him about the stained glass Jesus—how it had been put there when the church building was first built nearly 30 years earlier, how the artwork served as a memorial for one of the founding families in the church, how many of the older folks felt drawn into the presence of Christ through the light coming into through the window. My friend had unintentionally offended the family of the deceased member and had created an environment that distracted from worship, all from putting up a curtain on a stage.

"I'm telling you this story because churches are organic systems, and you have to be able to think in systems in order to make significant changes - even ones that don't seem quite as significant to you. When leading up, you must understand the system you're a part of."

"What do you mean by organic systems? And why was it somehow wrong for your friend to put up a curtain? Shouldn't the people just get over it?"

"See, you're thinking in a linear pattern, Logan. Organic systems don't operate on a linear level. With your service idea, you're thinking A + B = C."

Caleb grabbed one of the many napkins on the table, pulled out a pen, and quickly scribbled down a formula:

$$A \rightarrow B \rightarrow C$$

"Here's how you're thinking: A) Our church doesn't serve the community > B) The junior high kids love serving at the food bank > C) Our whole church should serve at the food bank on a Sunday. That sounds great, but it's never quite that simple."

"Okay, so how *should* I be thinking?"

"A church is an organic system, with parts that are interconnected and interrelated, making up a greater whole. Scripture calls this the "body of Christ," meaning that it's a whole body made up of various parts. When one part of the body is affected or changed, it has implications for the rest of the body. Sometimes those implications are quite dramatic, because systems are not simple formulas. A + B won't always equal C, because there is always a D, E, and F somewhere in the equation. You need to think in wholes, not formulas," Caleb said. He turned the napkin over and drew a new picture:

"This sounds really similar to our conversation about

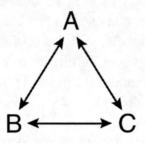

sacred cows," Logan said. "I told you about my conversation with Simon, right? About the gift drive? There was a lot more going on in the back of Simon's mind with the Christmas gift drive than I had originally anticipated. You're right, it's not so simple."

"It never is. Complex systems are, well, complex. I once heard a great metaphor for this in a book by Douglas Hall—it's the difference between a cat and a toaster."*

Logan nearly choked on his taco. "Uh, what?"

"A cat and a toaster. Cats and toasters have inherent differences, right? How you handle a problem with a toaster is very different than how you handle one with a cat. If your toaster is broken, you get out a screwdriver

---

* Douglas A. Hall, *The Cat and the Toaster: Living System Ministry in a Technological Age* (Eugene, OR: Wipf & Stock, 2010).

and some other tools and hope you can open up the machine and find the problem. If you tried the same approach with a cat, you'd end up with a dead cat and an angry phone call from PETA. Same thing if you wanted to create more systems or structure. With a toaster, you get an assembly line at a manufacturing plant and start mass-producing toasters. With cats, you just need a male and a female and the right romantic setting. You put two toasters in a dark room together and you're not going to get more toasters. The problem begins when we start treating cats like toasters.

"Hypothetically, let's think in organic systems about your Sunday service day proposal. How could a shift or change like that have implications on the whole system?"

Logan thought for a moment. "Well, for starters, it would mean that we would have a Sunday without a traditional offering. That has huge ramifications, especially if we didn't offer another way to give financially. Thinking about transportation—how would families get to where they need to serve? And would we have enough places to serve? The food bank was nearly overwhelmed by our junior highers this morning, so adding a few hundred more folks would be more harmful than helpful. Let's see…for the elderly folks, if they couldn't physically serve somewhere, they could feel excluded. And what about new people who visit that Sunday? Our local missions could backfire if a new person showed up to locked doors."

"See, and that's only the beginning," Caleb said. "There are both external and internal implications, ones that affect both the concrete and practical, as well as the emotional and relational. It's complex."

They paid their checks and walked outside into the bright Saturday sun. Standing in the parking lot, Logan had another question about the systems thinking Caleb had proposed.

"I'm playing a part in the system of my church in the junior high ministry. But I'm also realizing that God has placed this vision in my life that has huge implications for the whole church system. So, what do you think I should do? How do I remain faithful to both callings—the particular ministry I'm called to lead and the larger vision God has placed in my heart? I guess I'm worried that by pursuing the larger vision that I'll end up sucked into the complexity of the situation and lose sight of my immediate calling to disciple junior highers."

"Such a good question," Caleb replied, leaning on his car door. "How do you stay connected to the life of the body without getting sucked into the bureaucracy of church politics and policies? As an executive pastor, this is one of those tensions that I constantly have to navigate. If you start going off and doing your own thing—if you just started skipping Sunday morning church services in order to serve in the community—you'd end up without a job rather quickly. But if you get caught up in the complexity of the system without differentiating yourself from it, you lose yourself in the bureaucracy.

"The best way I've found to describe this comes from a book by Gordon Mackenzie*, who called this tension 'orbiting the giant hairball.' The hairball is the system, with its politics and complexity. It gives life, but it also has the ability to make you lose your individual identity and calling if you're not careful. Mackenzie offers that we orbit the hairball or that we live in the perfect tension of being connected to the system without being co-opted

* Gordon MacKenzie, *Orbiting the Giant Hairball: A Corporate Fool's Guide to Surviving with Grace* (New York, NY: Viking, Penguin Putnam, 1998).

by it. Think of the moon orbiting the earth; it has to stay at an exact distance to remain in orbit. Otherwise it flies off into space or crashes into the earth. This is a huge part of leading up, because you have to remain connected to the life of the system in order to implement change. Like the moon causes the tides, our connection in orbit allows us to have significant influence without being destructive."

"Orbiting a hairball and cats and toasters. You're full of metaphors today," Logan said.

"They may sound strange, but I guarantee that you're not going to forget any of them any time soon," Caleb replied. "On that note, I've gotta run. Evangeline needs me back home early to work on her car. The oil needs changing, and I'm certainly not paying some random mechanic thirty bucks to do an hour of work on my wife's car. I'll see you next week! Maybe we can try the enchiladas next time?"

Caleb leaned over and embraced Logan in a firm bearhug. It wasn't the first hug he'd received from Caleb, yet it startled him. There was strength behind it, a fatherly love that passed from Caleb to Logan in that brief moment standing in the empty parking lot. Logan stepped into his car and watched Caleb's truck drive away, grateful for the friendship that had deepened over the past year, and wondering if he could get Caleb to change the oil in his car, too.

Chapter Nine
Being Clint Eastwood

The youth room was a disaster. Logan scanned the situation, and then went to grab the cleaning supplies from the janitor's closet. A few volunteers were still chatting in the back of the room as Logan started to work on a particularly disgusting table. Grace had asked to use candles and crayons as part of some worship stations for the junior high worship night she had planned. Colorful wax was all over the tables and floors, mixing with spilled cans of soda to create a particularly sticky situation.

Logan quietly scrubbed as Grace put away music stands and equipment. He listened as she excitedly shared about the evening's events, how students drew prayers with the crayons, how they were jumping up and down during the last song, how the drummer broke a stick halfway through and it flew across the room. Logan glanced up at the hickory stick protruding from the wall.

"Why don't you come help me scrub the prayers off these tables?" Logan interrupted. "We can get the music stands later. Grab a rag and start cleaning."

Grace stopped abruptly, then sheepishly grabbed some cleaning supplies and started washing the nearest table. They scrubbed in silence for a few minutes.

"Logan, I know this is early to tell, but I'm wondering if we can make this worship night a regular thing, like maybe every few months. I don't think too many people give junior highers credit for their passion and excitement about the Lord. They really loved the whole night. I'd lead it; you wouldn't have to do anything besides come and worship. What do you think? I think it'd be awesome," Grace said.

I wouldn't have to do anything besides come and worship, and clean up after your mess, Logan thought.

"I dunno. Let's give it a week and think about it. There's a lot that goes into a night like this, and our calendar is already pretty full this year. Let's talk later," he replied.

Grace gave a brief nod in reply and kept scrubbing.

Man, she's got a lot to learn about this leadership stuff, Logan thought.

He was surprised that Ava was awake when he arrived home that evening. The youth room cleaning had taken far longer than he'd anticipated, and he was glad to see his wife after such an exhausting event. He dropped his bag, plopped down on the couch next to her, and closed his eyes.

"How'd it go?" she asked. He told her all about the crayons, the candles, the drumstick implanted in the wall.

"Grace wants to do these every month or something. I love her heart, I'm just not sure I want to commit to cleaning up messes and trying these crazy 'experiments' she's suggesting." Logan's voice sounded tired.

The silence caused him to turn and look at his wife, who was staring at him. "What?"

"Listen to what you just said, honey. Sound familiar? She's so excited about junior high ministry, she talks about it all the time with me. She's got a vision, Logan." She sat up and smiled. "Let's head to bed and talk about it more tomorrow. But take a shower first. You smell like Crayola and junior high boy."

***

"Hi there! We're here to check in. We're bringing some students lunch today."

Logan, Ava, and Grace smiled at the woman sitting behind the front desk of the academic office in the junior high building. She was on the phone, but offered a quick wave and smile in return. The boxes of pizza were hot and filled the office with a delicious smell of warmed cheese and pepperoni. Earlier that month, Logan had left voicemails and emails for each of the principals at the school. One assistant principal had returned his call earlier that week, and after a brief meeting over coffee, had agreed to allow Logan to come on campus once a week during the lunch hour to meet with students. "Check in at the front office, and no proselytizing," were the only requirements given.

Now Logan was here with a stack of pizzas in hand and a renewed spirit. The woman ended the phone call and turned her attention to the pizza-carrying trio.

"Who are you here to see again?" she asked.

"Hi, my name is Logan, and I'm the junior high pastor at Evergreen Community Church. I spoke with the assistant principal, Mr. McCarthy, this last week, and he gave me permission to bring lunch for some students from our church."

The front-desk woman eyed the three carefully, then pointed to a clipboard and pen sitting on her desk.

"Sign your names here, the time you arrived, and the purpose for your visit. You'll have to check out with me when lunch is over, and you'll need to wear these." She handed them nametags with the prominent moniker "Visitor" labeled above the blank space for their names.

After a quick scribble of signatures, the three were walking down the hallways of the junior high. The murmur of voices were audible as they passed each classroom, glancing quickly through the tiny rectangular windows to see if they recognized any students as they made their way towards the cafeteria. The lunch bell would ring in fifteen minutes and the hallways would be swarming with young teens scrambling to get to the front of the lunch line or find a seat at the conventional table of their cadre of friends. As they reached the end of the hall, Grace opened the large double doors with a brief nudge from her elbow and they entered the cafeteria.

Finding a large round table in the corner, they placed their respective boxes of pizza in strategic stacks that allowed the maximum amount of students to reach without causing a stampede. Then they sat down to wait.

"I'm so excited about this," Grace quipped. "I know you've been talking about getting out of the church building and into the neighborhood, Logan, but I didn't think it would actually be this...*easy*."

"Yeah, it did feel a bit easy, didn't it?" Logan replied. "All it took was a few phone calls and a bit of initiative on our part. And cost of a bunch of pizza."

Logan thought a moment. In one sense, this *did* feel easy. Yet he also recalled all the prayers and meetings and frustrations over the past year. Despite the simplicity of showing up at a junior high school with pizza, this had not been an easy journey for him. He wasn't sure he would have had the courage to explain the idea to Simon and Noah, to get Grace and some volunteers on board with the vision, to call the principals, and to show up today. *Humble confidence, he thought. This isn't about me; this always has been about you, Lord.*

"Thanks for inviting me to be a part of this," Grace said. "I don't know what it is, but I'm loving junior high ministry more and more every week. I feel like we're on the tipping point of something exciting here, even though it's just pizza. I'm so grateful to be a part of it."

"We're grateful you're here, too," Ava said. "And if you're both okay with it, I'm planning on stealing you away this afternoon and go for a hike out by the river. You can plan worship stuff for youth group later. Is that ok, honey?" she asked Logan.

"Yep, that's very okay. I didn't have any other tasks for you today, Grace. After this pizza frenzy, I was planning on going to do some teaching prep over a cup of coffee. Go for it!"

The two women smiled, and began joking about how Grace had to rescue Ava from falling into the river. Logan knew that these hikes were sacred times for his wife and his intern. The two had bonded deeply over this past school year, and Grace was feeling less like an employee and more like a part of their family. It was invigorating to see Ava pouring herself into a young woman, and to see Grace so eager to learn and grow from her.

"What do you both think this next season holds for our church?" Logan asked suddenly. "I'm just curious. You said it feels like we're at a tipping point, Grace, and I'm wanting to hear what you meant."

"I dunno," Grace said. "With the food bank experiment going so well, and now with this new connection with the school, it feels like the junior high ministry is expanding beyond the doors of our church. I'm noticing it with the students, too. They just seem excited about church, and not just because of singing worship songs or throwing dodgeballs at each other. I think they're starting to get it and really understanding what it means to live for Jesus beyond a Sunday morning or a youth group night. So, if that's true for the junior highers, I'm wondering if God is doing something more in our whole church through this." She motioned to the empty room and pizza boxes, and smiled.

Logan stared at Grace. The words felt almost prophetic, and they cut him to the core. He had mentioned his vision for local missions and social justice, but he didn't know that Grace had such a strong feeling in the same way. He glanced at Ava, who was also smiling. Logan thought she looked proud and content, but he wasn't sure if she was proud of Grace, of Logan, or both.

"Yeah that sounds really great! And hey, I'm sorry for cutting you off the other night when you were sharing about the worship night. I was tired, I apologize if I came off as a jerk. Your idea was solid, and I really want to talk it through," he replied.

Grace smiled. So did Ava. The lunch bell rang and the double doors burst open with students. A few eighth graders Logan texted earlier quickly scanned the room and made eye contact with Logan and Grace at the table. Moments later, a swarm of eager young adolescents were munching on pizza, laughing and sharing about their day with the three adults, each now wondering what God was doing in their midst.

***

Logan's cell phone buzzed in his pocket. A text message.

"Where are you?"

Caleb rarely initiated the text message conversations, unless it was to remind Logan where they were meeting that particular week. "I'm more of a face-to-face guy," he'd say.

"I'm at the coffee shop near Evergreen. What's up?" Logan texted in reply.

"Headed your way," was the response.

Ten minutes later, Logan saw Caleb walk through the door and turn immediately towards their usual table. "I'm over here!" Logan called. He was sitting on the other side of the shop, lounging in an oversized chair in a nook tucked away behind the coffee bar. Caleb grabbed a chair from a nearby table and carried it over, planting it down firmly in front of Logan.

"Everything okay, Caleb?" Logan was a bit worried about his friend's demeanor. Caleb was a straightforward and swift character, but he wasn't known to be impulsive like this.

"Yeah, everything is fine. Better than fine, actually. I was just looking over past journals and writings, and re-called something. You know what today is?"

"No, what's today?"

"It's our anniversary."

Logan peered at Caleb's face. The older man looked almost giddy, and Logan clearly wasn't getting it.

"A year ago today, I walked into this coffee shop and interrupted your angry email session. It's been a year, Logan."

Logan sat back. Memories from the past twelve months flooded his memory as he recalled all the frustra-tion and anxiety from that day, suddenly relieved by the intervention of his friend.

"Wow…I didn't realize. I'm glad you remembered. I'm feeling a bit nostalgic now," Logan said.

"It's been quite a year, hasn't it? And that's why I wanted to come see you, why this feels a bit spontaneous on my part. I wanted to celebrate our anniversary. I don't have anything mushy or corny in mind, and I'm not getting you flowers. I just wanted to take a minute to remember, together." Caleb paused, thought a moment, and continued.

"Logan, I don't know how this will sound, but…I'm proud of you. I'm proud of the man you are and the man you're becoming. All that insecurity and pride you were clinging to has practically vanished in the past year. You're a leader of humble confidence, one who leads out of his relationship with Christ and not out of techniques, experience, or job description. You're like a son to me. I'm with you and I'm for you. Don't ever forget that."

"Caleb, I don't know who I would be without you in my life. Thank you, for being my mentor in life. I'm starting to realize—maybe even in this moment, right now—how valuable and critical it is to have an advocate who walks alongside you when you're learning to lead up. Someone who is a sounding board, a wise and experienced leader who listens and speaks and guides and pushes and leads and serves. Thanks for being that advocate for me."

Caleb leaned back, placed his hand in his right pocket, and pulled out a folded note.

"This is better than a text message." He got up to leave and handed Logan the note.

"What, do I read this now?"

"Yeah, when I'm out the door. It's weird otherwise. I'll see you next week, Logan," replied the older pastor as he walked out the door and into the afternoon sun.

Logan waited until Caleb drove away then opened the folded note and read:

Logan,

Did you ever see that movie, "Gran Torino?" Clint plays a war veteran named Walt, who is this angry, gruff widower with a racist streak. One of his neighbors is a Hmong teenager named Thao, who one day tries to steal Walt's prize possession, a 1972 Gran Torino in mint condition. Walt catches the kid, and the two form a bond through the experience. Neither man realizes it at first, but they quickly become one another's advocate and mentor. Walt teaches Thao how to become a man, and Thao allows Walt to learn the way of grace. They grow more together than they could ever grow alone. Eventually, Walt gives both his Gran Torino and his life to make sure that Thao's future is secure.

I'm Walt. You're Thao. I've taught and guided you in the ways of leading up, but you teach me, too. I'm not planning on giving up my car or my life for you any time soon, but I'm telling you all this because I love you.

When Jesus was raised from the dead, He showed up to His disciples and told them this in John 20: "As the Father has sent me, so I am sending you." Later on, Paul told the Corinthian church to follow him as he followed in the ways of Christ. I'm telling you the same. Proud of what God has done in you this past year. Lead up, lead well, lead like Jesus.

Grace and peace,

Caleb

PS: You and Ava better keep mentoring Grace. That girl is gifted to lead. Let her.

PPS: Quit drinking that sissy coffee already and drink an Americano.

Logan set down the note with a smile. He stared at the floor for a moment, reflecting on all that had happened the past year. Realizing his coffee was cold, he got up, walked over to the barista, and ordered an Americano.

Chapter Ten

The Thorn in the Side

The following week, the rain pounded against the windows as Logan sat in the same coffee shop, staring at his phone. Caleb was supposed to be here, but he was ten minutes late. Logan would have to give a hard time to the ever-punctual mentor, who would chide Logan for being even a minute late to their meetings. The Americano Logan had purchased for Caleb was growing colder with the passing time. He watched the steam escape the lid, strong at first, then dissipating with swirls in the cool air. He would have to buy a new one when Caleb arrived.

Ten more minutes passed. Logan decided to give Caleb a call. The phone went immediately to voicemail, so Logan left a short message. "Hey man, just sitting here waiting for you to arrive. Hope everything is okay, give me a call or text me if you have to cancel today." Setting the phone down on his lap, a flash of worry swept through Logan's mind. He texted Ava about Caleb's tardiness, who told him to call Evangeline soon if he couldn't get a hold of Caleb.

Not wanting to waste the time while he waited, Logan called Grace, who was busy working on a new service project for the junior highers. Her role as a worship leader had quickly expanded over the year with her ambitious spirit, and she was eager to try leading her own small event by taking a group of girls to pick up trash at the local elementary school. They talked through the details of getting supplies and recruiting a few moms for transportation, with Grace furiously writing down notes on the other side of the phone.

When the call was over, Logan was surprised to realize that Caleb was over an hour late. The next call went to Evangeline. No answer. He called the church office where Caleb worked, and the assistant on the other end said that Caleb had left over two hours earlier, mentioning he was headed home before going to some afternoon meetings. Logan thanked the woman, then stared at the floor for a minute, thinking about his next move. He grabbed his bag, leaving both cups of coffee on the table, and jumped into his car.

Caleb and Evangeline's home was at least twenty minutes away from the coffee shop. The difficult drive on winding forest roads was compounded by the rain coming down, saturating the roadway and limiting vision. Logan's car zipped left, then right, then over a small hill only a few hundred yards from the driveway up to their country home.

As Logan came over the hill, the flashing lights of the ambulance were like shimmering red-and-white flares through the wet windshield. More lights were ahead. Logan peered through the rain to see several police vehicles and a fire engine. Two car lights were staring out from the surrounding forest at a strange angle, aimed skyward like unnatural spotlights trying to signal attention to this remote forest location. Logan pulled his car over with a hard jolt on the side of the road, got out, and splashed through the rain, sprinting towards the herd of emergency vehicles. Arriving on the scene, he saw that the two spotlights coming from the forest originated from a truck lying upside down on the forest floor.

It was Caleb's truck.

A police officer approached, telling Logan to get back into his vehicle. "I know that truck," he shouted. "Where is the driver? What happened? *Where is the driver?!*" Logan was becoming frantic.

"Logan!" He turned to see Evangeline approaching through the rain and police vehicles. He broke from the officer and embraced her with a hug. "What happened? Where is Caleb?"

"I'm…I'll tell you on the way. They just took him away in an ambulance…I need to go to the hospital right now, to be with him. Can you…can you come with me?"

The two ran to Logan's car while a police car escorted them towards the hospital. The details were still vague to Evangeline, but she did her best to share in between sobs. There was a stalled car on the other side of the hill. Caleb's truck had swerved to avoid it. The rain caused him to slide off. She didn't know any more, only that Caleb had been found inside the truck and needed immediate attention. They prayed desperate prayers and sped to the hospital, hoping for the best while fearing the worst.

***

Logan continued to blankly stare at the back of the pew in front of him as Ava gripped his hand. Her touch snapped him back to reality, and he looked down at the note Caleb had given clenched in his other hand. He wanted to be anywhere but this pew, but he knew that he had to stay.

The memorial service had just started.

The church sanctuary was completely filled with hundreds of people who had been touched by Caleb's life and ministry. There were clusters of people standing in the back of the room. Evangeline sat in the front row, directly in front of Ava and Logan, alongside her daughters and sisters. The tone in the room was somber, which annoyed Logan. He knew that Caleb would not have wanted them to feel this sense of loss and hurt, and that he'd want everyone to remember and celebrate the resurrection of Christ. Theology aside, the emotions were still present, and the suddenness of the accident left a large painful wake that no one anticipated. Caleb had died in a manner that was suitable to his character—abrupt, harsh, and for the sake of others. A young family from out of town was in the stalled car on the road that afternoon. They were lost and looking for the cabin they were supposed to vacation in. The reports said that Caleb had narrowly missed hitting the car, Their lives were spared by his swerve maneuver.

The memorial service was long, and the immensity of the emotional moment left Logan feeling strangely numb. Many family members, friends, and church members stood at the front to share about the beauty of Caleb's life. When it was time for Logan's turn to share, he prayed a silent prayer as walked to the stage with a confidence that only could have come from the Lord: *Help me, Lord. Help me.*

***

Weeks passed. The summer sun was a stark juxtaposition to the grief that continued to linger in Logan's heart. There were evenings where he would cry suddenly, when the tears would invade his eyes and spill out the pain that was emitting from his heart. Ava grieved with him; the two would drive to Evangeline's home often during those weeks, though her daughters and extended family stayed around to help with the details that come from a person's death. The moment coming over the hill towards the house was always a strange part of their drive. Such a familiar road had taken a surreal atmosphere. Logan dreaded the drive, but braved it for the sake of Evangeline.

Ministry still had to continue. Logan found himself finally laughing for the first time in weeks at a junior high summer camp, watching the students perform a talent show that involved a lot of lip-syncing and elaborate costumes. Logan had taken Caleb's written exhortation seriously and allowed Grace to take the majority of the leadership for the week. She stepped up naturally and led the group when Logan simply couldn't. The week of camp was refreshing for everyone, but particularly refreshing for Logan to escape the pain of ordinary life without Caleb. He came home renewed and eager, trying to focus all his emotions on his vision for local missions and justice at Evergreen.

In spite of the roller coaster of emotions Logan experienced in the past few weeks, the time felt right to approach Simon again with the vision. Fall was quickly approaching, and any new programs or ministry initiatives would need to be proposed soon in order to find themselves implemented in the next year. The week after summer camp was over, Logan knocked on the door to Simon's office.

"Come on in! How was summer camp?" Simon was in a good mood.

"Great, great. Lots of amazing moments of worship and conversations with the students about the Lord. And Grace did an amazing job. I had her lead a lot of our group discussions, as well as planning all the transportation for the trip. Plus, she just has a youthful energy about her. I'll be honest, Caleb's death has been so draining. Grace brings new life to the ministry. She's going places, Simon. I'm pretty proud of her."

"That's good, that's good," Simon nodded in reply. The two leaders caught up more on life and summer camp, as well as Logan's emotional well-being since the accident. Then Logan broached the idea of local missions.

"Simon, I've been processing a lot over this past year. I honestly feel like a new pastor, maybe even a new man. Caleb helped me a lot throughout the process, calling out me out where I was mistaken or thinking poorly, and offering a lot of new insights into leadership and what God is stirring in my heart."

Logan took a breath. "Do you remember the pastoral staff meeting we had over a year ago, the one where I offered a proposal about local missions to the team?"

"Yeah, yes. I remember," Simon said.

"Well, that vision hasn't left me. It might look different now than it did then, but the same passion and desire for local missions and justice has been a significant part of my thinking over the past season. You remember our conversation about the gift drive, and have certainly noticed the ministry experiment with the food bank?"

Simon nodded, leaning forward with intrigue.

"I've been trying to pursue that vision in my own context and ministry, and I'm watching God do amazing things. Students are growing in their faith, and our community is being dramatically affected by their willingness to serve and reach out to others. They're the public face of Evergreen Community Church to the neighborhood, trying to live out the Gospel that we value so highly. God is up to something in our community, and I think Evergreen should be a part of that mission.

"I'm here to re-propose my initiative, to ask you to look this over and prayerfully consider what local missions could look like at our church." Logan handed Simon a packet with the proposal.

"Sure, Logan. I'll look at it," Simon said. He took the packet and set it on his desk. There was a pause while Logan waited for Simon to respond. When he just quietly nodded and smiled, Logan stood confidently.

"Let me know what you think of the proposal, maybe we can talk next week?"

"Yeah, let's meet. Thursday morning work for you?"

"I'll check my calendar, but that sounds good to me! Looking forward to it."

Logan walked out the office, wondering about Simon's response to the proposal. He couldn't tell if it was positive or negative, but at least he was open to talking about it. But what if Simon rejected it again? Logan's heart sank. After all this time and effort, after all the coaching from Caleb and all the relational equity that Logan had built, after thinking through the systems of their church culture and recognizing some of the sacred cows, Logan was back right where he had started.

A smile. A nod. Possibly a rejection.

If Simon came back and talked with him about a calendaring system, Logan was going to quit.

***

The door swung open and Logan stepped into the coffee shop. He saw Evangeline already sitting in a chair, waiting for his arrival with two steaming cups of coffee set before her. She smiled her gracious smile, and stood up to give him a hug. Logan hadn't been inside the coffee shop since the accident. The place felt like a mausoleum, filled with memories of happier times and the sweet memories of Caleb's wisdom.

"You ordered me an Americano," Logan noticed.

"Well, you've got to learn how to grow up some day," Evangeline quipped, a smile behind her eyes. Her Caleb-like jab made Logan grin, partly because it was so out of character for Evangeline, and partly because it disarmed him. He had entered the shop with his defenses up, though not against Evangeline. He was protecting his heart from the emotions of the past. Nearly two months had passed since the accident, and the grieving process was still far from over.

"How've you been, Logan?" Evangeline asked.

"Good. As good as I can be. Ministry is coming together for the fall. Ava and I are talking about having kids sometime soon. It's all good, really."

Evangeline smiled. "How is it *really* going?"

Logan took a breath. She wasn't going to settle for small talk.

"I'm alive." The brief statement itself brought an emotion with it that surprised Logan. Tears formed in the corner of his eyes as he thought, *But Caleb isn't, and neither is my vision for Evergreen.* "I'm alive, and I'm tired, and I'm sad a lot of the time, and I'm frustrated with God, but I'm alive all the same."

"Me too. All of those things," Evangeline said with a tone of empathy. "I know that Caleb is in the presence of the Lord, that he's in a genuinely better place. I know that I'll see him again, and that will be a wonderful day indeed." She paused. "But I still want him here with me. I want him here for you, too. He loved you dearly, you know. We both do. To see you hurt like this breaks my heart, because I know that he would never want to see you suffer."

"That's exactly what this is— suffering. And even though it feels selfish and petty now, I'm just as frustrated with Simon and his response to my missions proposal."

"Oh, you shared the local missions vision again with him?" Evangeline probably knew all about the past year's journey from conversations with Caleb.

"Yeah, and it was the same response as a year ago. The smile-and-nod treatment. We're supposed to have a meeting later this week, but I'm not really looking forward to it. I don't think my heart can handle another episode of rejection right now."

There was silence for a moment, with Logan staring into the blackness of his espresso while Evangeline rested her head on her hand.

"There's always hope, you know. In Christ, there's always hope," she said after awhile.

"I know, like in my head...I just don't feel that hope in this season," Logan lamented.

"There is this passage in the book of Romans that you're probably familiar with, but it's taken the death of my husband to truly realize its significance." Logan looked up from his coffee as Evangeline leaned forward and pulled out her Bible.. "'Not only so, but we also rejoice in our sufferings, because we know that suffering produces perseverance; perseverance, character; and character, hope. And hope does not disappoint us, because God has poured out his love into our hearts by the Holy Spirit, whom he has given us,'" Evangeline read.

"Suffering leads to hope, Logan. That's an amazing paradox, and I won't pretend that I always feel this way.

But I *know* it's true, in my soul, in my heart. Our suffering will not be in vain, and God wants us to invite Him into our suffering in order to refine our character and give our hearts new hope."

Logan nodded thoughtfully. Evangeline continued.

"Whether it's the death of your friend and mentor, or the pain of having your vision rejected over and over again, there is always hope. It's not found in our ministry, or our vision for the church, or our personal comforts. It's found in Christ. When Caleb died, I thought my life was completely over. I had lost my heart, my will. His death only made me cling to Christ even more, because all else had been stripped away. My value and worth and purpose weren't found even in being the wife of Caleb; that was obviously important, but still temporary. Christ is eternal. That's why I can have hope in the midst of terrible suffering, because of Him." The honest confession was coming from the depths of her soul, and she wasn't going to stop now.

"There's another passage, one in 2 Corinthians, where Paul is talking about a thorn in his flesh. This thorn—whatever it is—is causing incredible pain for him, and he asks God to take it away repeatedly, to remove the source of pain from him. And God doesn't. He doesn't take it away. He leaves the pain. And Paul is left wondering, 'who is this God that I'm following, that allows pain in my life?' That's been my question too, and Christ actually responds to Paul directly: 'my grace is sufficient for you, for my power is made perfect in weakness.'

"Suffering is inevitable in life and leadership. If suffering leads to hope, and Christ's grace is sufficient, and His power is perfected in our weakness, then you and I are right where God wants us, Logan. It is awful and beautiful, all at the same time. Christ is both with us and for us, just like Caleb was with you and for you. I'm with you and for you, too. That's why I wanted to meet today; I wanted to remind you of who you are in Christ, because that's exactly what Caleb would be doing right now."

Logan looked at Caleb's wife and began to cry. She grasped his hand in hers and wept with him. In a small corner of a local coffee shop, two people suffered together and found hope together.

Chapter Eleven

Renewed Ignition

Logan entered his office swiftly and almost managed to close the door before Grace jumped inside. Today was the meeting with Simon, and Logan had a lot of preparation to do. Grace seemed eager to talk, and maybe her presence would take Logan's mind off the anxiety of the unknown of that meeting.

"Hey Logan, I've got a quick question to run by you. Well, maybe not quick, but a question," Grace said.

"What's up?" Logan replied.

"I know we need to have an official meeting about my internship at some point, but I wanted to ask you this now, because I'm trying to plan for the fall season. It's my senior year, and I'd still like to continue as an intern with you. I'm just wondering if you had thought about that yet, or knew what was happening so I could plan my schedule."

"I'm hoping you'll continue as an intern too! It's been a really great year of ministry together, and I know that Ava wants to keep you around." Grace smiled at that. "And I think you've got a lot to offer our ministry, and that you could still learn a lot from being here at Evergreen."

"Oh, good! Good. Okay, I'm glad. I've been praying that I could continue to serve here, I've fallen in love with junior high ministry, and I really like serving with you, and I've learned so much, and I hope to learn more!" Grace was clearly excited by the news.

"We can talk about it in more detail as the fall approaches, but yeah, I think you can count on having the internship continue for the next school year."

"Awesome! Thank you!" Grace gave an excited hug to Logan, and then bounced out of the room as quickly as she had arrived. As she left, a thought hit Logan for the first time—*Grace was not only a gifted leader, she needed opportunities to lead up.* He jumped to the door.

"Hey, Grace! Come back a minute!"

Grace had already made it halfway to the front door, but quickly turned around and bounded back to Logan's office, the smile never leaving her face.

"I'm glad you're so excited about the news, and I totally believe that you love junior high ministry, so I've got a question for you: what do *you* think we should do in junior high ministry this fall season?"

"Huh?" Grace was taken aback by the question. "What do you mean?"

"I mean, I want to hear what you think we should be doing in junior high ministry. I've been doing this for a while now, and I'm sure that the ministry needs fresh eyes and fresh ideas. I want you to feel the freedom to bounce ideas off of me. I'm officially inviting you to share ideas and to implement some of your own ideas as well. This can't just be *The Logan Show*. I think God has gifted you in some pretty amazing ways, and I bet He's stirring things up in your own heart for this ministry."

Grace thought a moment. "You know, I may have to get back to you. I've been writing down things in my journal all year, and I was so excited to lead that girls' service project last month. And I've got to run anyway, my friend is waiting in my car outside, but I just wanted to ask about this fall! We'll definitely have to talk! I've got plenty to throw your way!" Grace called as she ran out the door.

Logan grinned at her enthusiasm. She really was gifted to lead. *To really lead up, I've got to be willing to be led up*, he thought.

***

Logan walked into Simon's office and sat down across from the lead pastor. He was surprised to see two of the elders already present, Brian and Douglas. *Uh oh*, Logan thought. *This doesn't look good.* He didn't know that this would be a group meeting, particularly with a few of the key elders in the room. Adjusting in his seat, he wondered how quickly he could fire up his resume and send it out to local churches.

"Hey Logan, glad to see you. How is Ava doing?" Brian welcomed. The four men exchanged friendly greetings before Simon turned to business.

"Now, Logan, I know what you're thinking: you are *not* getting fired right now. Quite the opposite, in fact."

Logan breathed a deep sigh, relaxing in his chair, then immediately intrigued by Simon's latter statement. *Quite the opposite?* What was happening here? Simon handed him a stack of papers.

"Here is your proposal that you gave me, with an added proposal of my own."

Logan read the title to the top piece of paper: *Job Description: Pastor of Local Missions and Junior High Ministries.*

"It's a new job description for you, Logan. Your passion for local missions and loving our community in the name of Christ has been clearly evident since you were hired here. It's grown so significantly over the past year, and the entire elder board has been excited to see your personal growth in leadership. When you came into my office last week, I had already had a meeting with the elder board about a new job description for you starting by Christmas, but your proposal last week persuaded the elders and me to speed up the process. We don't want to get in the way of whatever God is doing in and through you."

"We really value what you're doing in our community," Brian said.

"You don't have to give an answer right away, but we'd love to hear what you think about the new job as soon as possible," added Douglas.

"Of course, this would mean a lot more ministry responsibility for you. You're probably already quite busy with the junior high ministry, and adding our church's mission initiatives and programs to your plate might be overwhelming. So this job comes with a raise in salary, as well as another new position," Simon said.

Another position? Logan wondered.

"We would want to make Grace more than an intern. We'd call her the director of junior high ministry, and make her full time at 30 hours a week. She would still report to you, but you would be able to hand off significant ministry responsibility to her, while still maintaining the level of maturity and health currently happening in junior high ministry."

Logan was speechless. Nearly eighteen months after his first proposal was shot down, he found himself with a new job, a new salary, and a new leader under his wing.

"I'll have to talk with Ava about it, but my initially reaction is yes! Of course, yes. And thank you! I'm so surprised, and so humbled."

"You're very welcome. We're excited about what God will do in this." Simon smiled and nodded, which made Logan laugh as he walked out of the office.

***

The bench was hard and cold, but Logan sat anyway. The breeze swept over the green grass of the cemetery, stirring up the fallen leaves into aerial dance that fluttered around the headstones. A few yards in front of him, a stone in the ground read the name of Logan's deceased mentor. Once a place of grief and dread, this bench had become a sort of sanctuary for Logan when he needed to process his own thoughts and ideas, particularly about leadership in ministry. Sipping on a warm Americano, he lifted his head to the sky and closed his eyes, the wind wrapping him up in its cool embrace as he offered a prayer of thanks to the Lord who had brought him here. *Where do we go from here, Lord? Where is Your Spirit guiding me?* He breathed deeply, filled with hope as he allowed the Divine to lead him up into the future and the mysteries of the kingdom.

Part 2: The Concepts

Leading Up

Introduction

I'm a leader in the church and I often don't know what I'm doing.

Don't tell anyone.

It's not that I'm completely clueless or incompetent. I believe God has both called me to ministry and gifted me to lead, giving me gracious opportunities that I'm not even sure I deserve. But I certainly haven't arrived yet. I'm still figuring this leadership thing out, still learning in the trenches of ministry, still seeking the Lord for what He would have next.

Maybe you're in the same boat with me. Whether you're a full-time pastor or a key volunteer, you likely picked up this little book because, like me, you love the local church. You want to see the body of Christ be an amazing Gospel community that loves God, loves people, and makes a significant difference in our world in the name of Jesus. But it's not there yet, and you have a God-given desire to see the church be changed into what it could and should be.

The only thing standing in your way: you're not in charge. There's a senior pastor or an elder board or a system or culture in your church that has the authority to make the changes you'd like to see. So you try to implement the changes in your own arena of influence, hoping someone will notice and ask you about your ideas. Or you make passionate pleas in staff meetings about the direction your church needs to go, only to seemingly fall on deaf ears. Or you drop subtle hints to your boss about an idea, praying he will get on board.

I've seen far too many church leaders silently frustrated with the direction their community is heading, but feeling helpless to stop it. They feel like they're standing at the front of a train with the brakes cut, seeing the wreck that is ahead and debating whether they can survive jumping off the train. Perhaps they have been shut down one too many times, so they quietly let the bitterness set in, slowly becoming cut off from other ministries and leaders. Or they stopped being silent and fervently shared their vision with anyone and everyone who would listen, only to get fired from the church for being insubordinate.

The common theme in these stories is the leader never learned to lead up.

I hope that Logan's story can be a source of inspiration and guidance in our struggles as church leaders to lead up. Leading up is an art, a skill that requires time and practice in order to feel like it's part of a leader's DNA. There's a lot at stake here. If we want to see the body of Christ functioning as God intended it, leaders in His church must learn the craft of leading up.

Chapter Twelve
The Who

Before leading up, you have to know who you are.

Who are you? How would you answer that question? Let me put some parameters on your answer—you can't answer with your job, your hobbies, your age, your family, or your marital status. Don't even answer with "I'm a Christian," unless you can unpack what that loaded word means.

So, who are you?

Let that sink in for a moment. While this isn't a book on identity formation, your identity will directly affect your effectiveness in leading up in the church. As Logan quickly learned, how he viewed himself and his ministry role clearly influenced his decisions and actions. When leaders in the church have built their identity on a temporary foundation—age or experience, ministry role, personal insecurities or strengths, job descriptions—it stifles how they will lead others. What happens when that identity foundation shifts or changes? How can someone lead when they're undergoing an identity crisis?

Like Logan, I built my leadership identity on who I wasn't and not who I was. At the onset of my ministry career, my identity was "the young church leader with a chip on his shoulder and something to prove." I didn't have the experience or gray hairs of my peers, but I wasn't going to let them judge me for it. Like a child trying to impress a parent, the driving motivation behind many of my leadership decisions were to gain the respect and attention of my elder ministry peers instead of actually pursuing the mission of Jesus in my life. When I shared my opinion, it was to make sure that the voice of young leaders was heard in my church. And if they didn't listen? Well, that was their loss! I thought I was a gift to their church, a young leader with maturity beyond his years, a key asset to the kingdom!

You can see the pride oozing from that last statement. My identity had been formed around my role, my age, my experience, and my own personal wounds. Jesus ended up getting tacked on to this tangled mess of an identity. It required a season of painful refinement for my eyes to be opened to the faulty foundation my sense of self was built upon.

You may be thinking, "isn't this incredibly basic and simple? You're just talking about finding your identity in Christ." Yes, it's basic, but it's not so simple. As church leaders, we can become blinded or jaded to the identity stowaways we may be harboring in our hearts. Look at the following statements; see if any resonate with your heart:

- "I'm a Christian (but I wonder if I'm really good enough for God)."
- "I'm deeply loved by a Heavenly Father (but I'm still trying to prove myself to him that I'm wor thy of his love)."

- "I'm gifted to lead and shepherd in the church (but I secretly don't like the people or pastors in my church)."
- "I have spiritual gifts that I use in leadership (but I'm not old enough/too old to really express them)."
- "I know the vision God has given me (but I also don't want to offend anyone or start any conflicts)."

I was once in a meeting with all the pastors and elders in our church where we were discussing the vision we had for our church for the next year. These were the key people leading our entire church community, and I was invited to be part of the conversation. Like many young leaders, I was frustrated with many aspects of our church's direction. So when the executive pastor specifically asked what I was thinking about our church's vision, there was moment of elation. I could make a difference! God put this opportunity right at my feet! They were asking me—the 20-something youth pastor—what I thought! So I ecstatically shared, pouring out my heart and describing where I thought our church needed to be.

They listened. And smiled. And nodded. And moved on in the conversation.

God used that moment to remind me that my identity and value does not stem from whether or not my ideas are approved by the people in the room. My identity and worth stems from Christ, and Him alone. To truly seek the approval of God and not people, I have to be willing to allow my own personal vision die so that Christ's vision for me can shine through. As leaders, we must begin to ask tough questions of ourselves. Who am I, really? Where is my worth found? What is my specific God-given calling in life? Do I love the vision I have for the church more than I love the Head of the church?

Self-Differentiation

In Edwin Friedman's excellent leadership book, *A Failure of Nerve*, he makes the revolutionary claim that the best leaders are not defined by technique or information, but by self-differentiation and presence. In essence, they are great leaders because they know themselves. In any sort of system, these leaders stand out because they remain calm and are not sucked into the dysfunction of others while still remaining connected to the system. Friedman uses the image of cellular biology that strong leaders are like a cell containing a nucleus and cell wall. They act as a sort of relational immune system, refusing to let the virus-like tendencies of others to sabotage them. Self-differentiation is a necessity to leading up. Friedman describes it this way:

> *Differentiation is not about being coercive, manipulative, reactive, pursuing or invasive, but being rooted in the leader's own sense of self rather than focused on that of his or her followers. It is in no way autocratic, narcissistic, or selfish, even though it may be perceived that way by those who are not taking responsibility for their own being. Self-differentiation is not "selfish." Furthermore, the power inherent in a leader's presence does not reside in physical or economic strength but in the nature of his or her own being, so that even when leaders are entitled to great power by dint of their office, it is ultimately the nature of their presence that is the source of their real strength.*

---

* Friedman, 230-231.

When a leader's identity is completely founded in who they are in Christ, someone is completely defined. Christianity is unique in that our identity is a gift that is graced upon us, not an effort of our own existential exertion.

Insecure Pride and Humble Confidence

Part of this identity shift and self-differentiation leads us from insecure pride to *humble confidence*. I'm aware that this sounds paradoxical. Think of them as two sides of the same coin. Insecure pride comes from focusing on oneself, on struggling to maintain one's own value and worth and identity without the strength of Christ. The insecurity comes from a personal anxiety, a self-doubt that comes across as a deflated or detached leadership. It is feeling unsure about oneself and what you offer as a leader to others. Connected with this insecurity is pride, an inner desire to make oneself and one's agenda heard in order to compensate for the insecurity. Pride often comes out externally through our mouths, while insecurity hides itself in the internal reaches of our hearts.

Insecure pride can manifest itself in all kinds of ways:

- Loudly and brashly sharing one's opinions in con versations in order to feel significant or heard.
- Not inviting any input on decisions that affect multiple people. Ignoring criticism or feedback, especially from peers.
- Offering unsolicited input and advice, especially to other leaders, then being personally hurt or of fended if they don't go with your idea.
- Choosing not to speak up around other leaders

due to an insecure fear of being wrong or uncertain.

- Choosing not to speak up around other leaders due to a prideful smugness that says, "no one else here could understand my ideas."
- Storing up bitterness against those who don't think like you do, speaking of them sarcastically or negatively when they're not around.
- Often making comparisons between themselves and other leaders.
- Their knee-jerk reaction shows self-preservation and defensiveness.
- Believing failure is not an option.

Take an honest inventory of your life. Do any of the above characteristics ring true in your recent experience? If they do, you might need to take some time to repent.

There is a healthier alternative paradox in leadership: the paradox of humble confidence. Humility comes from a realistic view of oneself in light of the grace given us in Christ. The word originates from the Latin "humus," meaning "earth, dirt." It is knowing and embracing the reality that we are dust (Psalm 103:14). Connected with humility is a confidence in one's vocational calling and identity. A confident leader finds their identity in Christ, seeing his or her self as a child of God, deeply loved and called to His mission. We're loved dust. This Christ-based identity allows His love to foster a confidence in Him, knowing we are created in His image and any gifts, strength, or opportunities we have are a demonstration of His grace in our lives.

Humble confidence may look like this:

- Quietly yet firmly sharing one's opinions when one discerns that they need to be shared for the benefit and encouragement of others and the accomplishment of the mission.
- Inviting honest feedback and evaluation, a willingness to be held accountable.
- A posture of listening and a desire to hear others' story. Offered advice comes from a desire to encourage and strengthen others.
- Choosing not to speak up around other leaders due to discerning spirit that is leading towards silence and contemplation in that moment.
- Seeing the good in others, even ones who don't think like you, knowing they are created in the image of God. Finding at least one thing to praise in another person.
- Doesn't have time for comparisons due to an intense focus on the mission they feel called to pursue.
- Their knee-jerk reaction is self-sacrifice for the sake of others and the mission.
- Believing failure is an opportunity for growth.

Insecure pride comes from attempting to form my identity and calling in myself and by my own efforts. Humble confidence comes from forming my identity and calling outside of myself through Christ. It is allowing Christ to be King, to shape my desires and ambitions instead of trying to build them myself.

In Jim Collins' *Good to Great*, there is a fascinating chapter on what Collins deems "Level 5" leadership. Looking at the CEOs of consistently successful companies, Collins' research revealed that the typical idea of a

CEO—loud, brash, egotistical, self-driven, etc.—were not characteristics of the best business leaders. The ego-centered CEOs were deemed Level 4 leaders. Level 5 was something else, where a humble sense of self was combined with a passion for the mission of the company. Collins puts it this way:

> *Level 5 leaders channel their ego needs away from themselves and into the larger goal of building a great company. It's not that Level 5 leaders have no ego or self-interest. Indeed, they are incredibly ambitious—but their ambition is first and foremost for the institution, not themselves ... Level 5 leaders are a study in duality: modest and willful, humble and fearless. (pages 21, 22)*

While Collins is writing from the perspective of the business world, we could replace the words "company" and "institution" with "church." To be humble and confident requires placing the value in the community and the mission, not in self-preservation. It's not that these leaders are weak or lazy; they simply don't require the flashiness or attention on themselves. One CEO summed up the differences this way: "The show horse and the plow horse—he [the Level 4 competitor] was more of a show horse, whereas I was more of a plow horse." Collins offers a great metaphor for this placing of "mission and community over self" using an analogy of a window and a mirror.

> *Level 5 leaders look out the window to apportion credit to factors outside themselves when things go well (and if they cannot find a specific person or event to give credit to, they credit good luck). At the same time, they look in the mirror to apportion responsibility, never blaming bad luck, when things go poorly.*

* Jim Collins, *Good to Great: Why Some Companies Make the*

This style of leadership sounds a lot like Jesus. When his authority was questioned in John 5, Jesus replied with "the Son can do nothing of his own accord, but only what he sees the Father doing." Jesus was constantly serving others, placing others' needs about his own, all the while on a deliberate and purposeful mission from the Father. Jesus was no pushover or weakling; neither was he domineering or power-hungry in his leadership. He is the Servant King, who made himself nothing, taking the form of a servant for the sake of the mission, yet highly exalted and above all other names on earth (Philippians 2:7, 9). He could do all this because his value and identity were not found in his role as Savior, nor out of comparison to other leaders, nor out of a desire to foster more attention for himself. He did it all out of a deep love for the Father, empowered by the Holy Spirit, and dying for the salvation of the world. Jesus never had to wonder "who am I?" in his leadership—he was the Son of God incarnated in our world, and he led accordingly.

It turns out that when self-differentiated leaders embrace humble confidence as their modus operandi, they become leaders who can be led up. No longer will you feel threatened by emerging leadership or innovative ideas that didn't stem from you. With humility, you'll realize that other leaders have just as much passion as you, knowing that God is also working in and through them to shape His church. When a leader's identity is found in Christ alone and the confidence they have springs from the mission of God, they are eager to see new or young leaders rise up and lead the church into new territory. Logan learned to allow Grace to lead him; we must learn how to be gracious as others lead us.

Leap...And Other's Don't (New York, NY: HarperCollins, 2001), 35.

As Logan began to realize that he had been operating from insecure pride, his entire perspective and approach to leadership had to change. In some ways, he began to share his ideas more, only with a humble and gracious tone. In other ways, he had to practice the discipline of not having the last word, choosing instead to prayerfully seek what the Lord was doing in any given moment. This takes time and practice; humble confidence doesn't happen overnight. If we're to be leaders who lead up, it must become a part of our very DNA, a central mantra in our leadership values. All of this describes a sense of being in the world, an identity and self-worth that is wrapped up in Christ.

Know who you are. Find your identity in the One who created you. Like Caleb told Logan, you are a masterpiece created by the Great Artist. Live from that identity.

Chapter Thirteen

The How, Part 1

I recall my first day in the office at my first ministry role. Previously an intern, I had been hired as the middle school director at the church where I was serving. I showed up, got keys to the office, and climbed the stairs to where the student ministry offices were located. Stepping into the new office, I sat down at the desk and briefly stared at the computer in front of me. The offices each had large windows opening up to a common gathering space, and I stared out the glass at the offices around me. Administrative assistants and pastors all were furiously working on some project or on an urgent phone call.

I sat there. No phone calls. No projects. Not even an email account set up. All the middle school students were in school. My calendar was completely open and free. What was a new pastor supposed to do?

I grabbed my bag, left the office, and went to go eat a slice of pepperoni pizza at my favorite local pizza joint. That first day, I didn't know what I was supposed to do, but the freedom due to ignorance wouldn't last long. My calendar has been full ever since.

After you know who you are, what do you do? Having one's identity established in Christ is absolutely critical to leading up. Yet we also require a set of tools on our leadership tool belt that help us to lead up effectively. You've heard about each of these tools in Logan's story, so I want to unpack some of the ideas and principles for how these tools will help you lead up better.

Relational Equity

If you've been doing ministry for any amount of time—or if you're a living human being—you know this foundational truth: *relationships matter*. We are designed and created for relationship and community. We inherently know this because being lonely or rejected feels awful, while having a sense of belonging and connection with others makes us feel alive. The God we worship is inherently relational, a singular Being in three distinct persons who unite in a divine dance of love and glory. Everything we do as leaders in the church comes back to our relationships with God and people.

This is part of our language as church leadership. Particularly popular in leadership circles today is the concept of *team*. Everyone talks about how we value the team and how we must trust one another in leadership and not allow our ministries to be silos. Nobody would argue with this concept; the value of teamwork has been praised since we received awards for *Playing Well With Others* in kindergarten class. Yet leaders in the church so often allow the relationships they have with their fellow leaders—teammates—to go by the wayside or never be established at all. Many of the motives for these relationships that are established are political ("I'm going to have coffee with the children's pastor for this next month so I can ask to use some of their budget for my summer camp supplies.") personal motives ("I think the worship pastor is really innovative and cool and likable, and I really want others to associate me with him, so I'll buy his lunch this week."), or pragmatic ("I'm going to ask the elder board to increase my salary this year, so I'm going to make sure I call each of them this week.").

The sad truth is that while the church praises relationships, many of the relationships between church leaders are shallow or nonexistent. Many are marked by mistrust, hurt, or a sense of competition. I have had enough frustration-laden conversations with friends in ministry to know that a truly healthy sense of team in a church's leadership is a beautiful rarity.

This is why relational equity is so vital to a healthy team. Picture all of the relationships you have as a leader within the church—all of the pastors, all of the elders or lay leadership, support staff, the volunteers, parents, and students. Imagine that each of these relationships is a bank account. You can make deposits into this account through a variety of ways: quality time spent together, words of encouragement and affirmation, acts of service and gifts, and even a supportive physical touch.· Each of these relationship accounts is both unique and interrelated; a deposit or withdrawal in one account may have an effect on another. Take a minute and write down the specific leadership relationships you have at your church. How much relational equity have you deposited into each of these accounts? How do you know? Relationships are mysterious and constantly in flux, but you can make

---

* Gary Chapman, *The 5 Love Langues: The Secret to Love that Lasts* (Chicago, IL: Northfield Publishing, 2010).

fairly accurate assessments on the depth and health of a particular relationship simply through evaluating how much you've personally deposited in the relational bank account.

Deposits are typically all healthy, but withdrawals from a relational bank account can have both positive and negative connotations. A negative withdrawal is fairly obvious—any breaking of trust or intentional harm quickly causes relational bankruptcy. While deposits always take a significant amount of time and patience to build an investment to a mature level, it only takes one misstep to completely bankrupt a relationship. Imagine a marriage built on love and trust for years suddenly experiencing the ripple effects of a spouse having an affair. Picture the youth pastor who has faithfully served at the church sending out an angry and slanderous email about the church senior leadership due to a recent financial decision they made. Envision the relational destruction caused by sharing the secret sexual struggles of a volunteer with the rest of the volunteer team and students. These types of withdrawals are usually fatal to relationships.

Not all withdrawals have to be destructive. On the contrary, Scripture reminds us that the wounds of a friend can be trusted (Psalm 27:6). On a personal level, this looks like privately confronting a close friend on their sin or exhorting them to make a difficult decision that needs to be done. On a leadership level, sometimes a vision from God requires the withdrawal of relational equity due to the dramatic change and implications involved. Canceling a beloved church program, embarking on a financial campaign, or calling church members to a deeper level in their faith and service may actually sting the listeners. This is the difference between causing pain and causing harm. Pain is like the knife of a surgeon; it is required for relationships to grow in healthy ways, particularly if there is something cancerous in one or both parties. Harm is like the knife of a murderer; it is destructive and crippling, causing relational ripple effects that can harm others.

Saying difficult things or having a radical vision will require relational withdrawals. Caleb had to call out Logan for his lack of initiative in the tension with Simon, and it hurt them both for a while. If the relational bank account is not full enough, these healthy withdrawals could bankrupt the relationship. But if time and energy has been spent building into the relationship, it not only can survive a withdrawal, but also may transform into a significant future deposit once the difficult season has been traversed together.

I've read literature that says true relationships cannot have an agenda, but I would contend that all relationships and actions always have some sense of agenda or motivation. I heartily agree that many unhealthy relationships exist due to manipulative agendas or hidden motives, using the relationships as a means to an end instead of an end in itself. However, instead of having *no* agenda, allow me to propose the *only* agenda worth having: love. Leadership relationships in the church should be characterized by love. After all, Jesus declared that the world would know Him in seeing our Christian love for one another (John 13:35).

Do you truly love your senior pastor? Do you really love the other pastors and leaders in your church? I'm not talking about tolerance or indifference or being nice. Jesus never called us to be nice; He called us to love one another as He loved us. I'm talking about sacrificial action, placing their needs and desires above your own in order to see them thrive and more fully live. If you don't love the pastors, elders, deacons, volunteers, parents, or students that you rub shoulders with in your church community, pray for the love of Christ to transform your heart so that you might fully love those around you. Love is the greatest deposit one can make in a relational bank account. A Christ-like love never loses value and always gains interest.

Sacred Cows

In a former church, we used to have a program every Christmas called Christmas Alive. We built an entire live Jerusalem in a grassy area on our property, complete with buildings and costumes and animals. There were Roman soldiers, the shepherds and wise men, and one lucky infant that portrayed the Christ child for a few evenings each December. The vision was to create an outreach program for the neighborhood, that they could come and fully experience the Christmas story.

For the first few years, Christmas Alive was fantastic. The people of our church had a creative outlet and community-building project in order to reach the people of our neighborhood, who were quite intrigued by this enormous setup in the middle of our grassy retention basin. New people came to know Jesus, the church members were actively serving and rubbing shoulders together, and all was well during the Christmas season.

Then something changed. Christmas Alive began feeling dead. The set designs were getting worn down from use, but no one had the desire to rebuild them. After years of participation with little-to-no change, a sense of apathy came over the volunteers. They became less interested in staying in character as ancient Jews or talking with the newcomers, and more interested in hanging out together in the cool evenings. The whole thing had lost vision and heart. Yet it remained alive in our church for a few more years because some vocal congregants believed that "we've *always* done Christmas Alive." Christmas Alive had become a sacred cow.

Every ministry has sacred cows. They are the programs, values, and ideas that can never be questioned because "we've *always* done it this way." These cows block the road to progress, forcing leaders to either bypass them completely or halt the implementation of a God-given vision.

Sacred cows typically didn't start that way. Most began as a God-given vision for change and growth in a ministry. That vision gained momentum, grew in its structure and reach until it became a church program. The program became part of the church's culture, with other visions and programs having work around it. At some point along the way, the program became more important than the God behind it (though the sacred cow worshipers would never admit to this). Sacred cows often go unnoticed until someone bumps into them and asks them to move or change.

Sacred cows are considered sacred because people have created an emotional connection with them. In some ways, part of their very identity is wrapped up in the program. When a person lacks self-differentiation—when their identity and value is intertwined in the cow rather than Christ—it leads to a far greater emotional backlash when those cows are questioned or tipped over. This is particularly true for the leaders and creators of the sacred cow. You're not just questioning the program; for them, you're questioning their leadership and their self-worth.

Leading up requires the tipping of sacred cows. I'm not usually a fan of the idea of "killing" the sacred cows right away, though it may be necessary later on. Killing sacred cows—shutting down the program immediately—shows a lack of systems thinking and how changing a single program can affect the community. If the creator of the sacred cow has their identity wrapped up in the program, you may think you're doing them a favor by killing the cow. But this is akin to haphazardly cutting someone open to try to remove a cancer. There are other ways that could do less harm and allow for a stronger re-covery, with the same results.

Instead of killing the cows, try tipping them. Expose them for what they really are—church programs, and nothing more. You could take a combative stance and point out how stupid a program is and how the church needs to change it immediately. Depending on who is invested in the sacred cow, that move could quickly get you into hot water (or fired). Leading up to those who have created the sacred cow means you must build re-lational equity with them in order to make a significant withdrawal when you question the cow. Instead of having a "me versus them" approach, humbly walk alongside the cow worshipers and look at the cow together. Invite them to truly look at the history of the program or event and differentiate themselves from the sacred cow by af-firming their value in Christ alone. Slowly but surely, the tipping point will be reached. When the cow is tipped over, it is far easier to move around it or kill it.

What are the sacred cows in your church context? Maybe it's an event or program; maybe it's a policy or procedure; maybe it's even someone's role. Tipping those sacred cows is a risky maneuver, but one worth pursuing in order to make room for fresh vision and Spirit-led renewal.

Systems Thinking

If you've ever taken a biology class, you realize that our world is incredibly complex. Each individual cell within the human body is its own system, with a nucleus and mitochondria and cytoplasm and golgi bodies and all sorts of other weirdly-named things that forced me to open my high school biology textbook. If each individual cell is complex, how much more is our entire bodily system? Each member plays a significant role; each organism is somehow vital to the whole.

Churches are organic systems. The predominant New Testament image for the church is a body. There are individual parts, but there is also the whole body, the whole church. Like the apostle Paul wrote in 1 Corinthians 12 about the body of Christ, *if one part suffers, all suffer; if one part is honored, every part rejoices with it.*

Problems begin to occur when one part decides that it is the most important in the whole body. Its vision, its ideas, its agenda, its programs, and its budget all take precedent over the other parts of the body. Perhaps you have experienced other members of the body who behave and believe like this. Or perhaps you are that member. Every leader naturally believes in the vision and ministry they have been called to embrace. Whatever ministry it is within the church, an argument can be made that it is incredibly vital to the health of that church system. Yet this would be similar to saying that the heart is the most important organ in the body. What about the brain? What about the stomach? What about the skin? This latter part doesn't initially seem as crucial when compared to the former organs, but without our skin, we'd literally fall apart.

Healthy leaders combat the individualistic and linear thinking inherent in these beliefs by adopting systems thinking. *Systems thinking* is having a framework for thinking about and understanding the interrelationships, connections and forces that shape the life of an organic system. Systems are at work all around us, whether we realize it or not. Your family is a system. Your neighborhood is a system. The government is a system. Every church is its own system that is within the larger system of the global Church and the kingdom of God. Navigating these systems in healthy ways requires thinking in terms of wholes and connections, as opposed to linear individualistic thinking.

Systems thinking is vitally important to leading up because it allows leaders to truly see the implications behind the vision and ideas they are proposing. When you approach your senior pastor or a group of elders with a fantastic idea, but haven't been thinking in systems, the results are often shut down due to the lack of thoughtfulness for how this idea will affect the whole church. Even a relatively small idea could have huge implications for the whole system, just like one tiny cell's activities can affect the health of a human body.

How does a leader develop systems thinking? There are a number of disciplines that can be learned and practiced. First, ask "why" questions. *Why do we do things this way? Why is this new venture or idea better than how things have been done? Why would people reject the idea?* Asking why begins to unearth the underlying structures and assumptions in a system.

Second, view every situation through the lens of relationship. If every part in a system is somehow connected to each other, how does this vision or idea affect the other parts in the system? How would individual people be affected by this new vision or idea? Knowing how individual pastors, volunteers, and church members will respond is critical in making a systemic change. A leader must ask how much relational equity they have built with these individual people. Thinking through the relational implications of a decision allows leaders to have greater empathy in the decision-making process.

Finally, take action. Systems thinking doesn't mean sitting around thinking through every possibility in a situation, or trying to make every part of the whole happy and satisfied. A decision needs to be made, and vision needs to move forward. What systems-thinking allows is a perspective of each part and how it is affected, even if the decision may hurt an individual member or program.

These three practices—relational equity, sacred cows, and systems thinking—all have overlapping implications for one another. Think of Logan's vision for bettering local missions at Evergreen. He had to build relational equity with numerous pastors and leaders in order to implement the vision and prove its worth, not just for his own individual ministry, but also for the whole. In doing so, he had to overcome some of the leadership's underlying beliefs about local missions based on a negative experience from the past. He also had to show how the missions program he presented would affect the rest of the church as well as tip the sacred cow of Evergreen's annual gift drive. If Logan had adopted a posture of individualistic and linear thinking, he would have ended up disconnected from the whole; he would have become a church tumor, using the resources of the body for growing his own vision and ideas. Church tumors either kill the body or end up being removed. Leading up with grace and a humble posture of systems thinking allows for leaders to avoid becoming church tumors.

Leading up ultimately comes back to relationships. How healthy is my relationship with those leaders who are leading our whole church? What are the important relationships and connections between ministries and church members? Striving for healthy relational connections—both personally and systemically—allows for church leaders to lead well as they lead up.

Even if you adopt all of these postures and practices, leading up doesn't always end well. There is no formula or guarantee. What happens when leading up seems to fail? We'll explore that question in the next chapter.

Chapter Fourteen
The How, Part 2

Leading up requires having a mentor who can be a sounding board for your ideas and an accountability partner who will lovingly guide you in your leadership journey. This advocate may be another leader within your own church, it could be another pastor at another church in your community, or it could be a professor at a local college or seminary. I would not be the leader I am today were it not for my mentor's input and guidance in my life. Timothy had Paul, Elisha had Elijah, Logan had Caleb. Find your mentor and advocate. You'll be a better leader for it.

The only reason I have any sense of knowing how to lead up is because a church leader, Mark Staples, once allowed me to lead up to him. I was in college and a volunteer in his youth ministry, mostly because my girlfriend (now wife) knew Mark from her hometown. After a year of volunteering, Mark invited be to become an intern with him, leading the junior high ministry. Mark didn't treat me like a typical intern; this wasn't a "go fetch me some coffee" or "go clean up the church basement" sort of role. I was barely twenty years old and Mark placed me in a role of significant ministry responsibility. Moreover, Mark invited me to offer feedback and input into his own ministry and leadership. He paced alongside me in life and allowed me to lead up to him. He was both a mentor and an advocate; he was with me and for me. He let me lead and shape the ministry, but also held me responsible for my mistakes, and offered wise input along the way.

Find an advocate and become an advocate for other leaders. Being led requires the same humble confidence as leading up. It requires valuing the whole body of Christ and the priesthood of all believers to all your vision and ideas to be shaped by someone younger, less experienced, or less knowledgeable. Yet if I cannot allow myself to be led up by another leader, then I am clearly missing the entire point of this book. It's not about me; it's about Christ and His vision for His church. That vision has been shared through anything from elderly prophets to burning bushes to talking donkeys. When God speaks, I want to be listening, no matter who He uses to be His microphone.

***

Let's say you are a leader who has found a humble confidence stemming from an identity found in Christ. Your significance doesn't come from your role or experience, but from the God who has called you to lead and given you a vision and passion for the church. You have built solid relational equity with the other church leaders, particularly the senior pastor. You have an understanding of your church's system and culture, knowing and evaluating the sacred cows in your context. You have found an advocate and mentor to come alongside you. Everything is ready for you to be a great leader within your church.

What happens when leading up still doesn't work?

I remember sitting down for lunch with the leader of my past church's men's ministry. The church had been struggling with numerous systemic flaws and sacred cows, much of it stemming from unhealthy church leadership. Caught in the middle of all this, I was deeply hurt and frustrated by the direction our church was headed. I could tell that this fellow leader was just as tired and drained as I had become. Since he had been in his role longer than I had been in mine, I wondered asked him how he continued to lead in this environment.

He replied (and I paraphrase), "I'm still here because I think God can still change things, but when you've been beating your head against a brick wall, eventually it's going to knock you out."

There is an aspect to suffering in leadership that is not often addressed in most leadership literature. They offer formulas and ideas and tools that will surely make you a better leader. But we know that this sort of linear and formulaic thinking doesn't work in real life.

In Romans 5, the apostle Paul makes a startling paradoxical statement that has huge implications for church leaders:

> *Not only so, but we also rejoice in our sufferings, because we know that suffering produces perseverance; perseverance, character; and character, hope. And hope does not disappoint us, because God has poured out his love into our hearts by the Holy Spirit, whom he has given us.*

Paul, suffering leads to hope. It produces perseverance and character, and this causes us to rejoice out of the love that God has poured into our hearts. This steadfastness and integrity in leadership can only come from a complete trust in the God who loves us. We are to ultimately be guided by the Holy Spirit, not by leadership principles found in a book.

Leading up entails sufferings. I don't want to lie to you; being in church leadership is not all fun and games. You will suffer long nights of wondering if your vision is even from God. You will suffer frustration at the hands of bureaucracy and church politics. You will suffer from people who question your authority and leadership capacity due to your job description, age, gender, or experience. You may suffer the pain of being fired. You may suffer from broken relationships and a deep doubts about the goodness and faithfulness of God. Remember that this suffering has the power to transform your character, to allow you to become an even better follower of Jesus, which will in turn make you a better leader in the church. Invite Christ to enter into the suffering with you. In Psalm 23, the Divine Shepherd leads the sheep through the valley of the shadow of death - not around, not away from, not over, but through the valley. On the other side wait green pastures and quiet waters and the calm rest of the soul.

Suffering leads to hope. This transforming from suffering to hope doesn't happen overnight. It requires patience and endurance and grace. Remember that truth when you're ready to throw in the towel.

Chapter Fifteen

Keep the Towel

Maybe you have been frustrated with the direction your church was headed. Maybe you have tried to step in and make some healthy changes, offering new ideas and direction for a church that was heading for disaster. You have stood in front of that speeding train with the brakes cut, and you refused to jump.

Then the train crashed.

Maybe you were blamed for the destruction, becoming the scapegoat for everything that went wrong. Maybe other leaders pushed you off the train, and you were fired from your job. Maybe you were tasked with fixing the wreckage, despite it being unsalvageable and not your immediate responsibility.

Whatever the case, you have been hurt as a church leader. Whether it was angry members of the congregation, betrayal from a pastor, or a disillusioned and controlling board member, someone or something in the church knocked you to the ground and left you there to bleed.

Maybe you have picked yourself up, but you still

have those wounds and don't trust the leadership in your church. Maybe you lead with a chip on your shoulder, not caring what others think and doing your own thing, because they just don't get you. Maybe you quietly sulk, wishing others knew the pain you have experienced, but afraid to share that with other leaders out of fear what they'll do or say. Maybe you are ready to give up, and this book was your last effort to see if there was any hope.

I've been there. I've sat in front of senior pastors and elders with tears in my eyes, hearing them make empty promises or completely ignoring my pain. I've seen friends in ministry get chewed up and spit out by unhealthy church leadership. I have had that chip on my shoulder, and have wondered if this whole ministry and leadership thing wasn't for me. Maybe God or I had made a mistake with this vocational calling.

Hear me: *do not give up*. Remember Jesus. There is infinite hope found in Christ, and He has promised to be with you always. This is His church and it's His body, and He is ultimately responsible for keeping it alive and going. He is also the one who transforms peoples' hearts; we are just the curators and guides along the journey, graciously invited to be a part of God's redemptive mission in our world. Christ suffered deeply too, and by His wounds we are healed. Through that suffering, Christ offers you comfort in the midst of your pain.

When I am discouraged, I have to come back to the specific vocational calling God has revealed in my life. It's not about my own frustrations, nor is it about my personal triumphs. My motivation must stem from outside myself in the mission God has invited me to join. Think of the prophet Jeremiah who was called by God at a young age to be God's voice to His people. Jeremiah preached and prayed and prophesied for his entire life. The result? No one listened, the people continued their downward spiral into sin, and ultimately were dragged away into exile while Jerusalem burned.

Was Jeremiah a successful leader? Not by our standards. Zero converts, tons of sinners, and the building burned down. Was he faithful and obedient to the calling God gave him? Yes. That has to be our standard for success as a leader in the church.

If you are thinking about throwing in the towel, hang on to it. Remember Jesus. Remember your calling. The Father of our Lord Jesus Christ is the Father of compassion and the God of all comfort, who comforts us in all our troubles, so that we can comfort those in any trouble with the comfort we ourselves receive from God (2 Corinthians 1:3-4). Keep leading up, and see how the Lord leads you and His church into a wondrous new kingdom reality.